D1175976

SOCIALISING PUBLIC OWNERSHIP

SOCIALISING PUBLIC OWNERSHIP

Martyn Sloman

First published 1978 by
THE MACMILLAN PRESS LTD
London and Basingstoke

Associated companies in Delhi
Dublin Hong Kong Johannesburg Lagos
Melbourne New York Singapore Tokyo

Printed in Great Britain by
R. & R. CLARK LTD
Edinburgh

British Library Cataloguing in Publication Data

Sloman, Martyn
Socialising public ownership
1. Government ownership – Great Britain
I. Title
338.6   HD4143
ISBN 0-333-22640-2

For my friends in the Labour Party,
especially those in Leominster and Bosworth

Contents

Preface

The second half of the part of the Labour Party's Constitution which is popularly known as Clause IV refers to the need for 'the best obtainable system of popular administration and control of each industry or service'. The 1970s have witnessed a resurgence of interest in public ownership in Britain and a renewed commitment to the principle within the Labour Party. Yet almost all of the debate has been concerned with the case for or against extending the public industrial sector. The practical problems surrounding the control of the industries have received far less attention.

This book is concerned with the development of the best forms of organisational structure and operational rules for common ownership. The options that are available will be set out and the possible choices outlined. Since all the major parties, irrespective of ideology, accept the need for a large public sector, it is hoped that the exposure of these alternatives will be of general interest. However, at the outset I feel that I should make my standpoint clear to the reader: my values are those of a mainstream member of the Labour Party who supports public ownership both in theory and in practice. I have spent the last ten years working in a major public corporation.

I have used the word 'socialising' to denote the process of changing the industrial system in a way that brings a positive gain to workers, consumers and the community. Nationalisation must become more than simply a vesting of ownership in the state. In my view this must be achieved by recognising explicitly the conflicts of interest that are inevitable in any industrial situation. Another idea that is central to this book is that more varied patterns of common ownership will be required in the future – this may well prove unacceptable to those who seek a single solution for all industrial problems.

The book falls into three distinct sections: background, argument and recommendations. Chapter 1 examines the place of public ownership in the Labour Party's political philosophy and Chapter 2 the post-war performance of the nationalised industries. The gap between theory and practice is identified. Chapters 3–6 develop the argument by considering the role of the workers, three organisational case studies, some causes of the underlying conflict and the deficiencies of some common panaceas. My proposals for change are set out in Chapters 7 and 8.

I owe a debt of gratitude to my employers for allowing me to write what is, at times, a book which is critical of the existing pattern of nationalised industries. I have been able to take advantage

of a set of guidelines for staff which is remarkably tolerant to those
who are politically active. These guidelines state that the corporation should not be named but I am grateful to it and, in particular,
to my present and previous managing directors. It would clearly be
undesirable if the development of the Labour Movement's policy
were left entirely in the hands of those who have no experience of
nationalisation in practice.

I should also like to acknowledge some of the people who have
provided valued advice and criticism. John Edmonds, Mike Elstob,
Bruce Grocott, MP, David Heald, Leslie Huckfield, MP, Professor
Anthony King, Lewis Minkin, George Mitchell and Frank Smith
have all helped to shape my ideas, though, of course, this does not
imply that they necessarily agree with my arguments or conclusions.
Two librarians, Sandra Simkin and Philip Toms, went to great
lengths to assist me by providing background reading and references.

My wife Anne did much more than merely cope with the reduced
social and family life that resulted from the long hours that I have
spent reading, assimilating and writing. Her support gave me the
confidence to embark on the project and the determination to finish.
Finally, my thanks to Julie Wyatt and Ann George who typed the
manuscript; Julie is amongst those to whom the book is dedicated.

MARTYN SLOMAN

London, October 1977

Abbreviations

BNOC	British National Oil Corporation
BSC	British Steel Corporation
BTC	British Transport Commission
CEGB	Central Electricity Generating Board
EEC	European Economic Community
EETPU	Electrical, Electronic, Telecommunication and Plumbing Union
GMWU	General and Municipal Workers' Union
ILP	Independent Labour Party
IRI	Istituto per la Ricostruzione Industriale
IWG	Institute for Workers' Control
KME	Kirkby Manufacturing and Engineering
LPACR	Labour Party Annual Conference Report
LPTB	London Passenger Transport Board
LRC	Labour Representation Committee
NCB	National Coal Board
NCC	National Consumer Council
NEB	National Enterprise Board
NEC	National Executive Committee (of the Labour Party)
NEDO	National Economic Development Office
NFC	National Freight Corporation
NUM	National Union of Mineworkers
POUNC	Post Office Users' National Council
SCNI	Select Committee on Nationalised Industries (of the House of Commons)
TGWU	Transport and General Workers' Union
TUC	Trades Union Congress

1 The Labour Party and Clause IV

Forty years ago, in his book *The Labour Party in Perspective*, Clem Attlee wrote these words, which speak to us as clearly as on the day he wrote them. This is what he said:

'The dominant issue of the twentieth century is socialism. Socialism is not the invention of an individual. It is essentially the outcome of economic and social conditions. The evils that capitalism brings differ in intensity in different countries, but the root cause of the trouble once discerned, the remedy is seen to be the same by thoughtful men and women. The cause is the private ownership of the means of life; the remedy is public ownership.'

We have not heard that sort of language for well over a generation.

[Tony Benn, Labour Party Annual Conference, 1975]

There are only two statements of aims in the Labour Party's Constitution. One is an open-ended promise 'generally to promote the political, social and economic emancipation of the people, and more particularly of those who depend directly upon their own exertions by hand or by brain for the means of life'. The second is the sentence, popularly known as Clause IV, which commits the Party to common ownership. The adoption of Clause IV marked the acceptance of socialism by the Party. To many of its supporters and opponents since then the Labour Party's concept of socialism has virtually been synonymous with public ownership.

Following the adoption of the clause the Labour Party has undergone a whole series of public arguments about the extent of its commitment to common ownership as an abstract idea – while persistently sidestepping the important issues concerned with the operation of publicly owned industries. The political debates, although important to the development of the Party's philosophy, have given an obvious impression of disunity. By avoiding an examination of the central questions of the organisation and control of public ownership, the Party has allowed itself to be identified in the public eye solely with the creation of large public monopolies. Its electoral popularity has inevitably suffered as a result of both these tendencies.

In some sections of the Labour Party today, political virility is measured by the degree to which the member can express the depth of his commitment to Clause IV. Labour Cabinet Ministers may periodically issue a statement reaffirming support for the mixed economy and a healthy and profitable private sector. No one who wished to court popularity would assert this at a local Labour Party meeting. However, as an examination of the history of politics

before the First World War demonstrates, socialism has not always
been so completely identified with nationalisation.

Many of the political antecedents of today's Labour Party, while
they were most definitely opposed to capitalism, would not be likely
to favour the centralist model of public ownership which currently
commands support. Amongst these groups must be numbered adher-
ents of the Owenite co-operative principles and also supporters of
workers' control. On the other hand, many advocates of public
ownership around the turn of the century did so on pragmatic
grounds and should not be regarded as socialists. In fact, the adoption of Clause IV by the Labour Party in 1918 was a victory for
one political group: those who wanted to make the movement a
socialist body in the distinctly centralist tradition which was
fashionable at the time. It was a hard-won triumph.

The Foundation Conference on Labour Representation, held at
the Memorial Hall in Farringdon Street, London, on 27 February
1900 witnessed both the first attempt to persuade the movement to
accept a firm commitment on public ownership and the first significant internal row. A delegate from the Social Democratic Federation, James Macdonald, moved a resolution which would have made
the movement's objective 'the socialisation of the means of production, distribution and exchange'. [Labour Party Foundation Conference Report (London), 1900, p. 11] By alienating the trade unions
such a full-blooded commitment to socialism could have severely
curtailed the growth of the infant movement and the resolution was
rejected in favour of a compromise which was far less precise. The
compromise was widely attributed to Keir Hardie, and it led to a
public dispute between Hardie's Independent Labour Party and the
Social Democratic Federation.

Further unsuccessful attempts were made to commit the movement to a socialist objective at the Labour Representation Committee Conferences of 1901 and 1903. (The movement did not call
itself the Labour Party until 1906.) The 1905 LRC Conference
passed a resolution which declared the movement's ultimate object
to be the overthrow of the present competitive system of capitalism
and the institution of a system of public ownership. This resolution was not treated as a constitutional amendment, however, and
in 1907 an attempt to incorporate this objective in the Constitution
was overwhelmingly defeated. Keir Hardie was amongst those who
spoke against, emphasising the potentially divisive effect on the
movement's Parliamentary supporters: 'Suppose this amendment
were carried. What followed would be that only men who were
Socialists could be Members of the Party in the House of Commons.
Did the movers of the amendment want to bring about such a
result?' [Labour Party Annual Conference Report (Belfast), 1907,
p. 52]

The Labour Party irrevocably became both socialist and a party with its acceptance of its new Constitution. This was considered and adopted by the 1918 Conference which began on 23–25 January in Nottingham and reconvened on 26 February in London. After the February Conference the Labour Party stood for the following object: 'To secure for the producers by hand and by brain the full fruits of their industry and the most equitable distribution thereof that may be possible, upon the basis of the common ownership of the means of production, and the best obtainable system of popular administration and control of each industry or service.'

This statement was adopted as Clause 3d of the Constitution. 'Means of production' was amended to 'means of production, distribution, and exchange', 'producers' was altered to 'workers', and the statement became Clause IV, para. 4, at the 1929 Party Conference. Otherwise it has remained unaltered as the enduring effective statement of the Labour Party's philosophy. The phrase 'the best obtainable system of popular administration and control' was a conscious political compromise and reflected an underlying difference of opinion which has remained with the Labour Party ever since. One group, the advocates of workers' self-management, have persistently sought to force a debate on the role of the workers under public ownership. They have exerted strong pressure to gain support for their viewpoint, but have generally been brushed aside – as was the case in 1918.

The 1918 Constitution was the work of Sidney Webb and a product of his collaboration with Arthur Henderson, who had become General Secretary of the Labour Party in 1911. Webb had become a member of the National Executive of the Labour Party three years earlier, taking the place of the General Secretary of the Fabian Society, who had enlisted in the armed forces. According to Edward Pease, himself General Secretary of the Fabian Society from 1890 to 1913, 'whenever Webb is on a Committee it may be assumed in default of positive evidence to the contrary that its report is his work.'

A draft of the Constitution was circulated together with a fuller statement of party objectives called *Labour and the New Social Order*. This document has been described as 'ostensibly the Report of a special committee of the National Executive but, with the exception of one or two paragraphs it is unmistakably the work of Webb'. [J. S. Middleton in his essay *Webb and the Labour Party* in Margaret Cole (ed.), *The Webbs and their Work* (London: Frederick Muller, 1949) p. 175] The section on 'The Democratic Control of Industry' contained in the document was misleadingly titled. Much of it was devoted to personal freedom, conscription, and electoral law. At the end of the section, however, there was a firm commitment to the abolition of capitalist control and the common ownership of the means of production. The document also contained one small reference to the organisation of the industries proposed for common ownership. This concerned the need for the 'adaptation, in particular services and occupations, of those systems and methods of administration and control that may be found, in practice, best to promote, not profiteering, but the general interest'.

The significance of this reference, and also of the second half of the new common ownership clause, can only be understood by examining the politics of the 1918 Labour Party. At the time there was a strong movement in favour of workers' control amongst the trade unions. The Miners' Federation, the National Union of Railwaymen, the Post Office Workers, and the Engineers were all to some extent sympathetic to the concept. There was division within the ranks of the ILP on their attitude. Webb, for his part, was implacably hostile.

In the most authoritative history of the time, G. D. H. Cole states that the Party Executive decided that it had gone 'quite far enough' to meet the demands of workers' control by referring to the best obtainable system of popular administration and control. The reference in *Labour and the New Social Order* is described by Cole as 'not only an evasion of the problem, but a statement of it in terms which implied, though did not positively profess, hostility to the claims of the advocates of workers' control'. [G. D. H. Cole, *A History of the Labour Party from 1914* (London: Routledge & Kegan Paul, 1948) p. 55]

Labour and the New Social Order was considered at a further Labour Party Conference held between 26 and 28 June 1918. Twenty-six resolutions were tabled in the name of the NEC in support of the document; none sought to clarify the section on the organisation of industry. This too, according to Cole, was deliberate. The matter was not discussed and the evasive statement was allowed to stand. The document remained the Party's major policy statement for another ten years. The pressure from supporters of an extension of the role of workers grew during this period, but the official position continued to be the compromise drafted by Webb. Towards the end of the decade the problem of implementing public ownership was no longer an academic one. The Labour Party was experiencing the difficulties of government and a choice had to be made on the most suitable form of organisation. This period witnessed the rare occurrence of an open debate within the Labour Movement on the pattern of public ownership.

Labour's first act of public ownership was the establishment of the London Passenger Transport Board. Herbert Morrison, Minister of Transport in the 1929 Labour Government, presented the London Passenger Transport Bill to Parliament in March 1931; its purpose was the unification of the disparate elements of the capital's transport system under a single board. When the Labour Government was replaced by the Coalition in August 1931 the Bill proceeded and, after some amendment, became law in June 1933.

Morrison was, therefore, the first Labour Minister faced with the practical problem of designing a form of organisation for public ownership. His choice was the public corporation – the form chosen for the Central Electricity Board in 1926. Morrison justified his decision in his book *Socialisation and Transport,* which the author's preface describes as 'Undertaken as an exposition of the LPTB the present volume has evolved into a study of the management of publicly owned industries generally'. [Herbert Morrison, *Socialisation and Transport* (London: Constable, 1933] At a time when 'Morrisonian' public corporations have acquired a degree of unpopularity in the Labour Movement, it is important to recognise the debt of gratitude owed to Morrison for producing such a valuable practical analysis of the problems of socialist organisation.

It was Morrison who popularised the term 'socialising' and, since it is used in this book's title, some clarification is needed. Morrison preferred 'socialisation' to 'nationalisation' to emphasise the social nature of the change that would be brought about by a transfer of ownership. Inevitably, like much of the vocabulary of Labour politics, the term has assumed a variety of different meanings. 'Socialising' is used in this book to describe the process of making public ownership more than the vesting of assets in the state; it reflects a view that public ownership should involve a direct gain to employees, consumers and the community. So far 'common ownership' and 'public ownership' have been used interchangeably – as they were in the Labour Party during the period under consideration. More precise definitions will be discussed in the next chapter.

The problem of organising publicly owned industries was seen, at the time of the establishment of the LPTB, as one of combining public accountability with a degree of management autonomy. Morrison argued:

> We have, I suggest, to find an organ of economic management and administration, not for all services, but for those of the more commercial – a word I am not using in the capitalist sense – and less routine character. It must be a public body; there must be public accountability of an appropriate form or forms; it must be efficient and speedy in action; it must have a social conscience; a corporate spirit and a public purpose; the legitimate right of the consumers must be safeguarded; so also must those of Labour in the industry.
>
> [*Socialisation and Transport,* p. 148]

These considerations led Morrison to adopt the public corporation

and he had wide support for his conclusion. Clement Attlee, who
had been Postmaster General in the Labour Government, had
written of the need for the Post Office to change from being a state
department to an organisational form showing the 'flexibility necessary in the conduct of a business concern'. William Graham, a
former Labour President of the Board of Trade, had spoken of a
steady transition to public corporations as the practical form of
socialism. Philip Snowden, Chancellor of the Exchequer in 1929,
had earlier spoken at Conference of getting 'our socialism very
largely in that way – that is through Public Corporations owned by
the public but controlled in the best interests of the public by the
best experts and businessmen whose brains and capacity can be
commanded'. [LPACR (Birmingham), 1928, p. 232]

Morrison begins his chapter on the 'Management of Socialised
Industry' by claiming that 'In earlier days it was assumed – perhaps
with more emphasis by anti-socialists than by socialists – that socialisation could only take two forms: State department nationalisation with the Minister responsible for management; and municipalisation under the Council and its appropriate committee'. [Ibid.,
p. 131] Here Morrison is being less than fair. Alternative forms of
organisation had been discussed, particularly relating to the coal
industry. Joint control, with workers in the industry participating
in management, had been a feature of Party policy since the presentation of the Miners' Bill to the Sankey Commission in 1919. In
1926 the Party had published a pamphlet called *Coal and Commonsense*, a popular version of the Party and TUC's evidence to the
Samuel Commission. This pamphlet proposed a complex scheme of
joint committees, composed of workers and officials, organised in a
hierarchical structure from an overall Power and Transport Commission down to colliery level.

Nevertheless by the 1930s State department nationalisation and
municipalisation had given way to the public corporation as the
favoured instrument of socialisation. In 1932 the TUC's Economic
Committee produced a *Report on Public Control and Regulation of
Industry and Trade;* Morrison was co-opted on to the Committee
and the following extract from the report amounts to a statement
of his position at the time:

The idea that socialisation and public control necessarily mean
administration directly by the Government department dies hard,
but is dying in every country. The importance of flexibility and
expert management on the one hand, and of freedom from party
domination on the other hand, has so far been recognised that
(as in the Labour Government's London Passenger Transport
Board) the tendency is to secure public control and the elimination of the profit motive while keeping the actual management

in the hands of a body not susceptible to party political pressure
and interference.
[TUC, *Public Control and Regulation of Industry and Trade* (1932)
para. 12]

Such opposition to the 'Morrisonian' public corporations that was
evident at the time came inevitably from the advocates of workers'
control. The main challenge to the 1932 TUC Report hardened on
the question of labour representation on public boards. The TUC
had supported this idea at its 1931 Conference; Morrison was irrevocably opposed. The Transport and General Workers' Union delegate at the 1932 Conference opposed the Report on the grounds of
the need for labour representation and the TUC General Council
referred the Report back to constituent unions. The dispute continued at the Labour Party Conference of the same year. Morrison
presented reports on Electricity and Transport which reflected his
insistence on appointment by ability alone; the TGWU moved
that certain members be appointed only after consultation with the
unions affected, and these reports were referred back for further
consideration. In 1933 a placatory memorandum, recognising the
right of the unions to consultation, was circulated by the Labour
Party's NEC and the TUC, but this was challenged at both Conferences. At the TUC Conference a General and Municipal Workers'
Union resolution which called for 50 per cent Board representation
for workers' nominees was passed and this eventually found its way
into the Labour Party's 1934 programme, *For Socialism and Peace*,
in the phrase 'the employees in a socialised industry have a right,
which should be acknowledged by law, to an effective share in the
control and direction of the industry'.

In fact, the Labour Party did not enjoy the opportunity of putting any of the ideas into practice until 1945. The General Election
of July of that year gave the Government the mandate to nationalise coal, electricity, gas, iron and steel, rail and inland transport.
The history of the period 1945–51 is the history of the industries
themselves, and a discussion of the relevant problems must wait
until later chapters. At this stage, it is worth observing that the
industries were all established as public corporations – and there
is no evidence of any challenge to this form of organisation.

The 1944 TUC *Post-War Reconstruction – Interim Report* had
stated unequivocally that, for each of the major industries, the
public corporation was the most suitable form of public ownership.
It quoted the section of the 1932 Report previously cited as the
justification for this view. The TUC orthodoxy on worker representation of the Boards was summarised thus:

In relation to corporations of this type, it is essential that res-

ponsibility to the public shall be maintained by the appointment
of the members of its governing body by a Minister responsible
to Parliament, and they should therefore be selected on the basis
of their competence and ability to administer the industry efficiently in the public interest. It is further essential that their
organisation shall make proper provision for the representation
and participation of workpeople, and to this end statutory provision be made for the interests of workpeople to be represented
on the Governing Board.

The demand for the statutory representation of workpeople was
never met as such, though workers in the industries concerned were
appointed to the Board. It is important to note that the demand
was for 'representatives' not 'delegates'; on appointment the workers' representatives would be expected to sever their connection with
the union. By 1945 the TUC General Council's Report to Congress
was able to describe the agreed views of the TUC and Labour Party
in the following terms: the two movements desired public control
of industry as such; since public control of industry was a means
towards efficiency, board appointments should be made on the basis
of competence and ability; statutory provision should be made for
the appointment of persons with knowledge of workpeople's interests, but care should be taken to avoid the creation of dual responsibility.

Labour's 1945 manifesto did not even mention the public corporation; it was implicit in all the proposals for nationalisation. The
industries were taken into public ownership in that form and 'experience of the organisation of workers' was built into the nationalisation Acts as a qualification for Board membership. It was almost
inevitable that early disillusionment with post-war nationalisation
centred round the role of the workers; putting a trade unionist on
the Board did not create socialised industry.

Dissatisfaction with the performance of nationalised industries
has remained a feature of Labour politics since 1945 and the role
of the workers in them has continued to provide the biggest source
of criticism. Despite this dissatisfaction there has been no thorough-
going debate in the post-war years on the organisation of the public
industrial sector. There have, however, been two major public rows,
in 1959–60 and 1972–3, about the extent to which the Party should
be committed to the principle of nationalisation. Both must be seen
in the context of the characteristic post-war behaviour of the Party:
simmering discontent with a Labour Government's performance,
building up to open rows when the Party is in opposition. These
rows generally take the form of an attempt by the fundamentalists
in the movement to blame the disappointments of office on a 'lack
of socialism'.

The defeat of the Labour Government in 1951 coincided with a recognition of the shortcomings of the public corporation as an instrument of socialist industrial policy, but this was not translated into positive proposals for reform. The 1950 policy statement *Labour and the New Society* had sought to persuade the Party to adopt a more varied approach to public ownership: 'In addition to nationalisation, public ownership can take many forms. There are different methods of serving the public good, which give the people more direct control over the sources of economic power.' These were listed as municipal enterprise, competitive public enterprise, voluntary co-operation, co-operative enterprise and the leasing of publicly owned factories and equipment. In the same year a group of left-wing Members of Parliament had issued a manifesto, *Keeping Left*, in which they argued that the public corporations had not provided everything which socialists expect from nationalised industry. *Keeping Left* pointed to the failure to integrate the corporations into national economic planning, the lack of parliamentary control and the failure of the arrangements for the representation of consumers and workers. The atmosphere was ripe for a wide discussion on the socialisation of industry.

Unfortunately, the discussion did not materialise. The left wing concentrated on the production of 'shopping-lists' of industries for future nationalisation; the right wing embarked on a review of the concept of nationalisation which ultimately resulted in an attempt to alter the Party's constitution. Neither tactic enhanced the prospects for socialised industry in any respect.

Shopping-lists are of particular importance to those who see a gradual advance to a totally public-owned industrial sector. Following the production of *Labour and the New Society*, which justified extensions of public ownership on pragmatic grounds, the left attempted to ensure that the next major policy statement included a specific list of industries to be taken into public ownership. In this they achieved some success: *Challenge to Britain*, published in 1953, set out a small list of industries that were to be nationalised, but a large list of industries in the engineering sector that were to be taken into partial public ownership. Attempts at the 1953 Party Conference to commit the Party to further acts of outright nationalisation were, however, unsuccessful.

The response to shopping-lists took several forms. The most important of these, echoing *Labour and the New Society*, was the promotion of alternative forms of public ownership to the public corporation. The Party Leader, Hugh Gaitskell, had in a 1956 pamphlet extolled the virtues of a more mixed economy with greater public participation achieved through ownership of selected firms within an industry and the extension of the activities of existing nationalised industries. [Hugh Gaitskell, *Socialism and*

Nationalisation (Fabian Tract No. 300, 1956)] Tony Crosland in his influential book had expressed similar sentiments:

> The ideal (or at least my ideal) is a society in which ownership is thoroughly mixed-up – a society with a diverse, diffused, pluralist, and heterogeneous pattern of ownership, with the State, the nationalised industries, the Co-operatives, the unions, Government financial institutions, pension funds, foundations, and millions of private families all participating.
>
> [C. A. R. Crosland, *The Future of Socialism* (London: Jonathan Cape, 1956) p. 496]

At the heart of what was by now a growing dispute within the Party was the suggestion that socialism could be achieved without all-embracing nationalisation. The phrase 'nationalisation as a means not an end', used by both Gaitskell and Crosland, was short-hand for this viewpoint. To the fundamentalist the abolition of privately owned industry was a necessary condition for socialism, if not a sufficient one; the distinction between means and ends was therefore blurred. The debate can further be characterised as one between those who justified extensions of public ownership by pragmatic arguments relating to the industry concerned and those who justified extensions of public ownership by arguments relating to the need for the economic control of industry as an instrument for achieving economic justice. Both sides in practice supported an expansion of public ownership; neither was happy with the performance of the existing public sector. The continuing controversy was therefore both damaging and irrelevant.

In 1957 the Party published a pamphlet entitled *Industry and Society: Labour's Policy on Future Public Ownership*. This publication was thoughtful, well argued, but thoroughly anti-fundamentalist. It opened with the sentence: 'Public ownership has always been regarded by British Socialists as a means towards achieving the ultimate ideals of socialism.' It included a sophisticated critique of private ownership; and it ended by restricting the likely extensions of public ownership to steel, road haulage, and 'any industry or part of industry which, after thorough enquiry, is found to be seriously failing the nation'. The analysis in *Industry and Society* was much bolder than its conclusions, but it was overwhelmingly endorsed by the 1957 Annual Conference.

In the same year a companion pamphlet, *Public Enterprise: Labour's Review of the Nationalised Industries,* was issued. Unfortunately, the complacent tone of this document failed to provoke any sort of debate in the Party. It specifically ruled out any changes in the public corporation form, in the arrangements for consumers, and in the method of parliamentary accountability. It rejected the idea of fuel and power councils, and of efficiency audits. Its conclusion included such anodyne recommendations as: 'As a general rule, Board members should have their terms of office renewed'; and 'In the field of labour relations the separation or otherwise of negotiation and consultation will vary from industry to industry depending on the circumstances.'

The tone of *Industry and Society* was echoed, almost verbatim, in the 1959 election manifesto. The opponents of fundamentalism appeared to have won the ideological battle; the subsequent actions of their Leader, Hugh Gaitskell, were, however, unquestionably damaging to their cause. His behaviour is difficult to understand, but it had its roots in the circumstances of the election defeat.

Six months before the election the Conservatives had taken the Labour proposal to extend public shareholding in private firms and used it to suggest that the Party intended to nationalise 500–600 large firms. Morgan Phillips, the General Secretary, was forced to issue a statement which sought to make clear the limited extent of the Party's commitment to further nationalisation. Despite this attempted clarification, it was widely agreed at the time that public ownership had lost the Party a great deal of support.

The election took place on 8 October 1959; a short Conference was held at Blackpool on 28 and 29 November. Hugh Gaitskell opened the debate on the General Election accepting that nationalisation had lost the Party votes. He attributed this to the unpopularity of the existing nationalised industries and confusion in the electorate's mind about Labour's future policy. Had he concentrated exclusively on the first problem he could have opened a debate which had been effectively closed with the publication of *Public Enterprise*. By attempting to redefine Labour's future policy on the expansion of the public sector, however, he embarked on a course which ended in a humiliating defeat.

After reviewing the existing industries Gaitskell stated that the only specific reference to objectives in the Constitution was Clause IV, para. 4. He argued:

Standing on its own, this cannot possibly be regarded as adequate. It lays us open to continual misrepresentation. It implies that common ownership is an end, whereas in fact it is a means. It implies that the only precise object we have is nationalisation, whereas in fact we have many other Socialist objectives. It implies that we propose to nationalise everything, but do we? ... I am sure that the Webbs and Arthur Henderson, who largely drafted this Constitution, would have been amazed and horrified had they thought that their words were to be treated as sacrosanct 40 years later in utterly changed conditions.

[LPACR (Blackpool), 1959, pp. 112–3]

Gaitskell subsequently claimed that his intention was to leave Clause IV, para. 4, unchanged but to add a new statement of aims to the Constitution. He failed to make this evident at the time and, if this was his intention, his remarks were ill-judged. At the 1959 Conference he was forced to sustain an attack from Frank Cousins, General Secretary of the TGWU, who declared: 'But if, as I gather, Rule 4 is likely to be revised to make a different reference to our attitude towards public ownership, I would suggest, with the greatest respect to our leader, that no way . . . is going to change that one.' [LPACR (Blackpool 1959, p. 131]

This dispute seemed likely to expire when the NEC met in March 1960 and accepted a Gaitskell draft which left the original Constitution intact, but added some points of amplification. However, several important trade unions, at their subsequent conferences, refused to accept this compromise. The NEC accordingly decided on 13 July 1960 not to proceed with any amendment or addition to Clause IV of the Constitution, but declared that the statement which it adopted on 16 March was a valuable expression of the aims of the Labour Party and commended it to the 1960 Conference accordingly. This statement was composed of twelve clauses including the controversial Clause j which reads:

> It is convinced that these social and economic objectives can be achieved only through an expansion of common ownership substantial enough to give the community power over the commanding heights of the economy. Common ownership takes varying forms, including state-owned industries and firms, producer and consumer co-operation, municipal ownership and public participation in private concerns. Recognising that public and private enterprise have a place in the economy it believes that further extension of common ownership should be decided from time to time in the light of these objectives and according to circumstances, with due regard for the views of the workers and consumers concerned.

These Gaitskellite sentiments were unacceptable to some sections of the Conference and over a third of the delegates voted in favour of a reference back. Since the reference back was defeated the statement technically remains a 'valuable expression of the Party's aims'. Gaitskell had however seriously underestimated the attitude of the Party's rank and file towards public ownership and received a rebuff. His statement of aims has long since been forgotten.

The continuing debate on public ownership entered a new phase in the 1960s with the wide acceptance of the view that the main justification for a state-owned industry was its use as a tool for national economic planning. This development is most closely associated with the period 1964–70, which saw a Labour Government under Harold Wilson in power. It had begun, however, when Gaitskell led the Party. In 1961 a major new programme, *Signposts for the Sixties*, included a section on 'The Role of Public Ownership' in a chapter entitled 'Planning for Expansion'; a decade earlier this relationship would almost certainly have been reversed. The 1964 Election Manifesto began its section on public ownership with the words: 'The public sector will make a vital contribution to the National Plan.'

The actual extension of the public sector promised in the 1964 manifesto was limited; this negative commitment was honoured. The endorsement of the use of nationalised industries as instruments of national planning, however, gave the Labour Movement a yardstick for judging the success of public enterprise. The industries did not meet the expectations of the Movement and, characteristically, disillusionment once again set in.

A return to fundamentalism was inevitable after the comparative failure of the 1964–70 Labour Government. Unlike 1959, however, the resurgence from the left did not take the form of a groundswell against those members of the Party who were less committed to public ownership. Nor could anyone blame the 1970 election defeat on nationalisation. A major public row did not materialise until the publication of the pamphlet on the National Enterprise Board in 1973.

This Green Paper was produced by the Labour Party's Public Sector Study Group, which was established after the 1972 Party Conference. The forceful presentation of the case for a State Holding Company set out in this document was a coherent articulation of views that had been circulating within the Movement for some time. Labour's adoption of the State Holding Company as an instrument for socialism reflected, in part, the growing admiration for the operation of holding companies in Italy.

As early as 1969 a National Executive Document had genuflected towards Italian experience:

> The dynamism and growth which characterises the Italian public industrial structure is completely missing from the British scene, and it is in order to develop this that over the past few years the Party has considered the establishment of a new State Holding Company along the lines of the Italian IRI. This could be the financial and managerial base for promoting new public enterprise, and could help to reassert what must be one of the primary objectives of regional economic planning in the years ahead – the promotion of a vigorous and expanding public sector.
> [*Labour's Economic Strategy* (1969) p. 40]

State holding companies had existed elsewhere: the Swedish Statsforetag had been particularly successful, but it was the Italian
model that attracted the Labour Party. Six public corporations are
organised under a Ministry of State Owned Industry: IRI, ENI,
EGAM, EFIM, EAGET, and Ente Cinema. IRI, which is the largest,
was founded in 1933 when the State was obliged to take over the
interests of a number of failed banks; it is a conglomerate with
wide interests in banking, manufacturing and service industries.

Stuart Holland, himself a member of the Public Sector Study
Group mentioned earlier, described IRI in the following way:

> Its inspired extension in the post-war period has provided
> Governments with a concrete example of what otherwise appeared
> difficult or impossible to achieve – state enterprise as efficient and
> dynamic as leading private enterprise groups, yet still directly
> serving the ends of Government economic policy and the inter-
> ests of society as a whole.
>
> [S. Holland (ed.), *The State as Entrepreneur*
> (London: Weidenfeld & Nicolson, 1972) p. 1]

Unfortunately the Italian public sector experienced a number of
management problems in subsequent years, many of which reflected
the uneasy underlying relationship between industry and state. In
1975 the Chairmen of ENI and EGAM were dismissed following
separate controversies: the ENI Chairman had a dispute with the
Industry Minister, who complained that he was receiving inadequate information on the company's activities; EGAM experienced
serious economic and political problems and eventually ceased
operations. In 1976 the Chairman of the shipping subsidiary of the
IRI resigned after a warrant for his arrest had been issued in connection with the Lockheed scandal.

The idea of a State Holding Company was attractive for a number of reasons. It was recognised that a more flexible form of
organisation than the public corporation was needed if public
ownership was to expand into the private manufacturing sector.
Government involvement could be kept at a distance and greater
managerial autonomy permitted if the shares in manufacturing
industry were vested in a holding company. Italian experience
proved it could be done. There was, too, a political advantage in
this form of organisation: it could appeal to all sections of the
Labour Movement. Crosland had argued in *The Future of Socialism* that, as the natural monopolies had been nationalised, the
future of public ownership lay in competitive public industry. By
1972 Roy Jenkins was able to develop this concept to argue the
case for the establishment of a State Holding Company as an instru-

ment of regional policy. [Roy Jenkins, *What Matters Now* (London: Collins/Fontana, 1972) pp. 31–7] From a fundamentalist standpoint Barbara Castle was able to give the idea a resounding endorsement in her 1971 Conference speech introducing the NEC policy statement, *Economic Strategy, Growth and Unemployment.*

It seemed in 1972 as though the Party could be embarking on a discussion on the sort of organisation that a State Holding Company should be. Once again what began as a useful debate degenerated into a public row. The 1972 Conference passed two resolutions which were rigidly fundamentalist in tone. The first began: 'This Conference instructs the next Labour Government to implement Clause IV in full.' The second asked the NEC to 'formulate a socialist plan of production, based on the public ownership, with minimum compensation, of the commanding heights of the economy'; and called for a 'plan for the democratic control of industry through workers' control and management'. [LPACR (Blackpool), 1972, pp. 175, 178]

This then was the mood when the Opposition Green Paper, *The National Enterprise Board: Labour's State Holding Company*, was published in April 1973. The document proposed establishing the NEB to achieve a more equitable distribution of industrial power, to act as a tool of regional policy, promote industrial democracy, and act as a counter-balance to the multinational corporations. It was an expansionist viewpoint, justifying the extension of public ownership by the need to achieve economic control through state ownership.

One passage in the Opposition Green Paper, however, dominated the ensuing debate. Although the document specifically rejected any attempt to draw up a list of candidate firms to be placed under the NEB it stated that:

About one-third of the turnover of the top hundred manufacturers, two-fifths of their profits and about half their employment should be vested in the NEB. Dependent on their size, the takeover of some twenty to twenty-five companies would yield control of an area of the economy of this degree, which we believe to be essential if the public sector is to exercise an effective role in economic planning. [p. 21]

The press had anticipated this hostage to fortune. Over two months earlier *The Times* had referred to 'a remarkable plan showing how a future Labour Government could take twenty-four leading public companies into state ownership' [5 February 1973]. On the day the Green Paper was published all the major newspapers concentrated on the twenty to twenty-five companies; later many of them included a list of likely candidates. The parallel with the events of April 1959 was almost exact.

A battle then ensued between the Shadow Cabinet and the NEC on whether the proposal should be included in *Labour's Programme for Britain 1973*, due to be presented to the October Conference. In May it seemed that the reference to a specific number of firms would be dropped, but, after a twelve-hour meeting the NEC decided, by seven votes to six, to keep the commitment. Harold Wilson, the Party Leader, did not vote but immediately afterwards issued a statement saying that it was inconceivable that the Party could go into a general election on this proposal. Roy Jenkins, who had recently resigned as Deputy Leader, gave his support to the Wilson veto.

The reference did appear in *Labour's Programme for Britain 1973*. In introducing the document to Conference Harold Wilson made his position clear:

> My own view on the 25 companies proposal has been stated. I am against it. The Parliamentary Committee is against it. I will leave it with these words, that the Parliamentary Committee charged by the Constitution with the duty of sitting down with the Executive to select, from the Programme adopted by the Conference the items for including in the election manifesto, entirely reserves its full constitutional rights on this matter, and there could be nothing more comradely than that.
>
> [LPACR (Blackpool), 1973, p. 167]

This paved the way for the compromise that appeared in the February 1974 election manifesto which referred to the creation of a powerful NEB with the structure and functions set out in Labour's programme.

The Green Paper on the NEB contained one commitment that was never fulfilled. The Public Sector Study Group reported that:

> In our work, we have been very much aware that public ownership carried with it special responsibilities. It is, or should be, ownership by the people. Yet the pattern of public ownership on the model of the public corporation has in the past seemed to workers within the industries themselves, to consumers of their services or products, and to the general public, to offer few advantages over private industry. There has been no new awareness of a new relationship between workers, consumers and the state as owner: for although very considerable efforts were made initially to create an institutional basis for new relationships, by setting up training schemes and consultative machinery, they have not succeeded.   [p. 10]

A special paper which would put forward new proposals was promised.

The special paper was never published, although it was also promised in *Labour's Programme for Britain 1973*. The February 1974 Election Manifesto contained a commitment to socialise existing nationalised industries: 'In consultation with the unions, we shall take steps to make the management of existing nationalised industries more responsible to the workers in the industry and more responsive to their consumers' needs.' This promise, which was not repeated in the October 1974 manifesto, had not been preceded by any sort of debate within the Party.

This chapter has sought to demonstrate the limitations of the public debates that have taken place since 1918 within the Labour Movement on public ownership. The disputes have been concerned with the extent of the Party's commitment to the abstract principle; the organisation of the publicly owned industries and the problems of socialising them have scarcely been raised. Morrison's *Socialisation and Transport* remains the one important organisational analysis.

Tony Benn, the Minister most associated with the Party's new position, paid tribute to Morrison's work when he delivered the Herbert Morrison Memorial Lecture on 7 July 1976. He concluded:

Herbert Morrison's achievement was a formidable one and history will record it as such. But it is now equally important that the Labour Movement should turn its mind to the transformation of these public corporations into expressions of our socialist purpose – namely that policies and institutions must serve the people and not become their masters. I am sure that Herbert Morrison himself would support our endeavours to improve upon what he himself had begun.

It is also true that Morrison – and Webb for that matter – would have been astonished at how little debate had subsequently taken place on the 'best obtainable system of popular administration and control' of publicly owned industry.

Chronology

1900 First Conference of the Labour Representation Committee.
1905 LRC passes resolution affirming socialist objective.
1907 Labour Party Annual Conference rejects attempt to add socialist objective to Constitution.
1918 LPAC adopts new Constitution including 'Clause IV'. *Labour and the New Social Order* published by Labour Party to clarify new socialist position.
1920 Webb's *A Constitution for the Socialist Commonwealth of Great Britain* published.
1929 Morrison appointed Minister of Transport.
      LPAC accepts minor amendments to Constitution.
1931 Morrison presents London Passenger Transport Bill to Parliament.
1932 *Report on Public Control and Regulation of Industry and Trade* published by TUC, endorsing the public corporation.
1933 Morrison's *Socialisation and Transport* published.
1934 *For Socialism and Peace* published by Labour Party, accepting need for employees to have effective share in control of industry.
1944 *Post-War Reconstruction – Interim Report,* published by TUC, advocates public corporations with statutory representation for workers.
1950 *Labour and the New Society,* published by Labour Party, argues case for more varied approach to public ownership.
1953 *Challenge to Britain* published by Labour Party. Includes 'shopping-list' of industries for partial public ownership.
1956 Gaitskell's *Socialism and Nationalisation* and Crosland's *Future of Socialism* argue case for nationalisation as a means, not an end.
1957 *Industry and Society* and *Public Enterprise* published by Labour Party: both are compromising in tone.
1959 Morgan Phillips, General Secretary of the Labour Party, issues categorical statement that Labour will *not* nationalise 500–600 large firms.
      Following election defeat, Gaitskell speaks at LPAC of need for clarification of Party's position on nationalisation.
1960 NEC in March accept Gaitskell draft as valuable statement of Party's aims.
      In June NEC decide not to proceed with any amendment or addition to Clause IV.
1961 *Signposts for Sixties,* published by Labour Party makes case for public ownership primarily as an instrument of economic planning.

1969 *Labour's Economic Strategy,* published by Labour Party, suggests creation of State Holding Company.

1972 Public Sector Study Group established by Labour Party. LPAC passes fundamentalist resolutions on public ownership.

1973 Opposition Green Paper, *The National Enterprise Board: Labour's State Holding Company,* which contains reference to nationalisation of twenty to twenty-five companies, published by Labour Party.

1974 Labour's February election manifesto contains commitment to socialise existing nationalised industries.

2 Public Ownership in Practice

> The Public Corporation must be no mere capitalist business, the be-all and end-all of which is profit and dividends, even though it will, quite properly, be expected to pay its way. It must have a different atmosphere at its board table from that of a shareholders' meeting; its Board and its officers must regard themselves as the high custodians of the public interest.
>
> [Herbert Morrison, *Socialisation and Transport*]

The intensity of the Labour Party's post-war debates demonstrates the central place that public ownership occupies in orthodox British socialism. The failure to undertake a parallel debate on the organisation of publicly owned industry has, however, created a gap between theory and practice. Quite simply there have been insufficient attempts to relate the organisation structure and the operational rules of the nationalised industries to the socialist ideas that are held by many supporters of public ownership.

The history of nationalisation in Britain is the history of a number of large public corporations. At the end of 1976 nine separate nationalised industries in the UK each employed more than 50,000 people: the Post Office, the National Coal Board, the British Rail Board, the British Steel Corporation, the Electricity Industry in England and Wales, the British Gas Corporation, the National Bus Company, the British Airways Board and the National Freight Corporation. The electricity industry, at a time when a Government decision on its reorganisation was pending, comprised the Electricity Council, the Central Electricity Generating Board and twelve Area Boards. Other nationalised industries employing less than 50,000 people were the British Airports Authority, the British National Oil Corporation, the British Transport Docks Board, the South of Scotland Electricity Board, the North of Scotland Hydro-Electric Board, the British Waterways Board and the Scottish Transport Group.

In the previous year, these nationalised industries taken together had accounted for 9·6 per cent of the nation's output, 6·9 per cent of its employment, and 14·4 per cent of its fixed investment. [*A Study of UK Nationalised Industries: Background Paper 3* (London: National Economic Development Office, 1976) p. 4] A Central Electricity Board was established by a Conservative Government in 1926 to operate and regulate the generation of electricity.

The airways were effectively nationalised in 1939. The steel industry was denationalised in 1953 and renationalised in 1967. The Post Office ceased to be a Government department and became a nationalised industry in 1969. The British National Oil Corporation was created in 1976. The major Acts of nationalisation, however, were introduced by the post-war Labour Government.

All these nationalised industries are organised as public corporations on Morrisonian lines, but the terms are not synonymous. A public corporation is a public trading body which has a substantial degree of financial independence from the Central Government. It has two main characteristics: the Government appoints the whole or the majority of the Board; it is a corporate body free to manage its own affairs without detailed control by Parliament and can maintain its own reserves. It is a moot point whether the application of the Bullock Committee proposals on industrial democracy to the nationalised industries would make them cease to be public corporations since, if the proposals were accepted, the Government would cease to appoint the majority of Board members.

Nationalised industries are more difficult to define. A 1976 NEDO study describes them as public corporations whose assets are in public ownership; whose Board members are appointed by a Secretary of State but are not civil servants; which are primarily involved in industrial or other trading activities; and whose revenue is derived directly from customers. The nationalised industries form far and away the most important part of the nation's publicly owned industrial activities. The Government also has a large shareholding in limited companies, either held directly or through the National Enterprise Board. In 1976 it owned both Rolls-Royce (1971) and British Leyland through the NEB and also it held a large number of shares awaiting transfer to British Shipbuilders. Government shareholding is growing in significance as a form of public ownership.

This excursion into the vocabulary of public ownership is important, not just for the sake of precision, but because it highlights an important theme that runs throughout this book. The gap between political theory and operational practice is reflected in the different terminologies: the operational terminology of the industries and the political terminology of their supporters are sometimes distinctly different. 'Nationalised industry' and 'public corporations' are terms which are used to define the actual organisation of industrial concerns; 'public ownership', 'common ownership' and 'socialisation' are used in statements of political position. Hugh Gaitskell used 'public ownership' to mean ownership by the community of any property, whether industrial or not, whether embracing a whole industry or only part of it; he used 'nationalisation' to mean the state ownership of a whole industry. 'Common ownership' has traditionally meant public ownership and other types of non-private ownership including co-operative and municipal ownership. 'Socialisation' has already been defined as the process of changing the industrial system in a way that brings a positive gain to workers, consumers and the community.

This chapter is concerned with the evolution of the industries as examples of public ownership, and will focus attention on the disparity between socialist theory and industrial practice. It is not concerned with the operation of the industries as economic entities in isolation from political considerations. The industries are of a scale and importance to have merited a number of economic and organisational analyses for which the political aspects of their behaviour were incidental. In this study they are central. The industries have also been the subject of a number of quasi-economic studies in which the political aspects of their behaviour was far from incidental: these studies were designed to prove that the industries have been inefficient and that this was an inevitable result of public ownership.

It is not intended in this book to go into any detail on how 'successful' the industries have been. However, some divergence from the main theme is required: the opponents of nationalisation are always far more vociferous than the supporters, so a small attempt to redress the balance is necessary. Since many of the public utilities have been the subject of almost continual criticism, it is important at the outset to recognise the many definite successes. The major fuel industries have coped with technological changes which posed enormous organisational problems. The electricity industry expanded the grid at a pace which compares favourably with any country in the world; no British city has ever known a breakdown like the one which plunged New York (served by the privately owned Consolidated Edison Company) into darkness in July 1977. The gas industry has undergone a total transformation following the discovery of offshore natural gas. The coal industry, and also the railways, have overseen a traumatic run-down in manpower in a humane manner whilst maintaining satisfactory industrial relations. The Post Office, which perhaps faces the biggest burden of criticism of all the industries, does in fact handle more postal items per employee, charge lower prices and deliver more letters the following day than the postal service in any other EEC country. These achievements are all the more remarkable when seen against the background of the confused policy for the industries that will be described later in this chapter.

Blanket assessment of the performance of the nationalised industries as a whole is, however, virtually impossible. The major nationalised industries are 'infrastructure' industries which carry a burden for the provision of services and, although this is often forgotten, for research and development, which is not shared by private manufacturing industry. Further, the inheritance left to the industries by the private owners was much more akin to a millstone than a legacy. The formulation of any yardstick for overall success is fraught with problems; adequate objective financial and economic indicators are simply not available.

Any attempt to assess overall performance based on the profit and loss account of the industries is inadequate, since they have never been allowed the freedom to charge the prices that they wished. *Background Paper 5* of the 1976 study undertaken by the National Economic Development Office contained a review of Government price restraint on the public corporations: for the decade 1965–75 no fewer than eight distinct attempts to restrain gas and electricity prices, six attempts to restrain rail prices, and five attempts to restrain postal prices and steel prices were recorded. The paper concluded that there was no evidence of price restraint on coal in the decade. Sir Derek Ezra, the Coal Board Chairman, in a letter published in the *Investor's Chronicle*, 12 December 1976, gave very positive estimates of the loss the NCB incurred as a result of price restraint in early periods; he estimated that the coal industry lost at least £2000 million of justifiable revenue in the first ten years of nationalisation, and £500 million in subsequent years.

The NCB did not receive any compensation for price restraint, although this has become standard practice in recent years. The industries have consistently claimed that the compensation that they have received is inadequate: the electricity industry, for example, claims to have experienced a shortfall of £1000 million between 1970/1 and 1975/6 as a result of restraint, for which only £500 million has been received from the Government. BSC have never received any compensation, though their Chairman has attributed a shortfall of £750 million in profits to the effects of price restraint between 1967 and 1976.

The effects of these constraints on the freedom of action of the industries have made it virtually impossible to judge their commercial performance. An alternative based on their operating performance is equally beset with difficulties. An important attempt was made by Richard Pryke, an economist who specialises in the problems of public ownership; in 1971 he tried to measure the technical efficiency of the industries and concluded that:

During the second decade of public ownership the sector's rate of advance (5·3%) has been much faster than that of private industry (3·4%) and manufacturing (3·7%). The only part of the public enterprise sector which has not secured a larger increase is the nationalised bus undertakings whose productivity has, like that of the private bus companies, declined. In contrast the only manufacturing industry whose productivity has increased faster than that of the public enterprise sector is chemicals.

[Richard Pryke, *Public Enterprise in Practice*
(London: MacGibbon & Kee, 1971) p. 434]

Pryke also argued that the productivity gains compared well with continental experience.

His views were well received by supporters of public ownership and evoked a noisy challenge from their opponents. However, when Pryke updated his work in 1976 he concluded that the performance of public ownership in the period 1968–73 was far less impressive:

> Output per equivalent worker continued to increase at a rapid rate in gas, electricity, telecommunications and airways. Indeed, all of these industries, apart from British Airways, made greater progress than they had during the previous five years. On the other hand British Rail which had pushed up its output per equivalent worker by 5.7% a year between 1963–1968 only had an increase of 2.6%. BSC and the NFC also had modest gains of about the same size, but in coal, output per equivalent worker was static and in posts there was a reduction of 1.4% a year.
>
> [*Guardian* 6 December 1976]

Pryke's work was a valuable attempt to make a comparison between different industries and between the same industries at different times. This is notoriously difficult. How, for example, can the performance of the National Coal Board be compared with the mining industry in North America, where strip or opencast mining predominates, or in the rest of the world, where geological conditions, a prime determinant of cost and revenue, are totally different? Before leaving this subject one further valuable study should be mentioned. In 1977 an assessment of the way that five major industries – gas, electricity, coal, telephones and European Airways – had managed technological change was published. The intention of the author, Chris Harlow, was not to provide an overall verdict on the management of change, but his study unquestionably reflected well on the industries' performances. [Chris Harlow, *Innovation and Productivity Under Nationalisation* (London: PEP, 1977)]

On balance, therefore, there is little justification for the strident criticism of public ownership; it is unfair and damaging to the industries. Much of this criticism has, in any case, resulted from the contradictory expectations that many people display towards nationalisation. The industries are expected to provide a high level of service, keep down prices and make a profit, though not an embarrassingly large one – even if it is needed to finance a major investment programme. These inherent contradictions were best illustrated at the times of the railway closures following the Beeching report in the early 1960s. Everyone was in favour of making the industry more profitable and efficient, until it meant closing their own local station or line.

These contradictory expectations have also been present in the minds of the supporters of public ownership and this explains, in part, why the Labour Movement has been less than vigorous in meeting attacks on the public corporations. The case for nationalisation argued by socialists has often been a mixture of general statements of socialist principles and the practical arguments for the public ownership of a particular candidate industry.

A number of separate strands of the traditional argument can be identified. The most important of these is the Marxist argument that a system of private ownership deprives the workers of the full product of their labour; closely linked is the notion that private possession of capital gives too much economic power to too few people. Other more pragmatic arguments are that public ownership is essential as a prerequisite to national economic planning and that certain services are natural monopolies and should be operated in the public interest. These pragmatic arguments are based on strong opposition to a system of allocation by a competitive market. A further set of arguments stress the potential improvement in working conditions attendant on public ownership. The relative importance of these different strands has varied over time. It is now a truism that much public ownership has been carried out to ensure the survival of basic industries: this has certainly applied recently to the nationalisation of Rolls-Royce (1971) Ltd and British Leyland. The major post-war battlegrounds have concerned the creation of the NEB, the British National Oil Corporation and, from an earlier period, the British Steel Corporation.

The political case for nationalisation has never been translated into hard rules for the operation of the industries when nationalised. An assessment of performance against criteria derived from the political arguments is therefore almost impossible. All too often an idealised expression of the socialist case for nationalisation, like the general public's demand on the industries, can only result in contradictory expectations. Contradictory expectations result in conflicting objectives.

The remainder of this chapter will be devoted to an examination of the methods of public-sector organisation and control since 1945. These have taken the form of minor alterations in the structure of the corporations and in the operational rules. The changes and other ideas proposed will be discussed in a broadly chronological order; but, at the outset, it should be stated that they have evolved in a piecemeal fashion. There have only been two occasions when it even looked as though a satisfactory overall framework for the operation of the industries had been established. The first was at the beginning of the period under review, when high hopes were held for the public corporation structure itself. The second was towards the end of the 1960s, when the combination of Government acceptance of non-commercial obligations and the introduction of pricing and investment rules opened a new era in public-sector policy.

The emergence of the public corporation structure as the 'answer' to the problems of organising public ownership has already been described. The corporations were intended to be autonomous bodies acting as a weapon of Government policy. The initial Acts of nationalisation contained two distinct attempts to ensure that the industries played the role that the Government desired: the first, and less important, was the specification of the objectives for the industry; the second was the power delegated to the Minister.

Almost all the nationalisation Acts contained an industrial objective which was sufficiently general and ambiguous to amount to almost no practical guidance. The Coal Industry Nationalisation Act 1946 charged the industry with 'making supplies of coal available, of such qualities and sizes, in such quantities and at such prices, as may seem to them best calculated to further the public interest in all respects, including the avoidance of any undue or unreasonable preference or advantage.' Similar provisions were included for the other industries; their main purpose was to give the industry a nominal commercial purpose, while specifically rejecting the 'capitalist' notion of profit-maximisation. The result was that interpretation of the objectives was left to the industries themselves. This was deliberate: The Minister of Fuel and Power, Emanuel Shinwell, argued during the Second Reading of the Coal Industry Bill: 'Who are better fitted to judge [the public interest] than the people who are running the industry?'

Some of the Acts also contained some overt non-commercial objectives. The Electricity Act 1947 required the Electricity Boards to 'secure so far as practicable the development, extension to rural areas and cheapening of supplies of electricity'. The Transport Act 1947 went a stage further in setting out a duty for the British Transport Commission to provide an integrated system of transport.

The Acts also outlined a financial target – which again required conduct which was commercial but not profit-maximising. The Boards were required to ensure that revenues were not less than sufficient to meet all outgoings chargeable to the revenue account, taking one year with another. The legislation also created Consumer Councils or Consultative Committees for the industries and placed specific obligations on them to consult and negotiate with their employees. Both these aspects will be considered more fully in later chapters.

The powers given to the Ministers by the Acts varied. The most important ones were: power to appoint Board members; power to approve capital investment and research programmes; powers of control over borrowing and use of reserve funds; power to give the Board a general direction in the national interest. Potentially the most important of these, the one instrument that could have made management of the industries subordinate to Government policy, was the power of general direction. In practice this has proved the least effective. As early as July 1947, Herbert Morrison, speaking in his capacity as Lord President in the Labour Government, told a Ministerial Committee on the Socialisation of Industries that it was generally agreed by Ministers that 'there should be as few general directions as possible'. In the following year the same Committee agreed that 'it is accepted policy that general directions should only be used in exceptional circumstances'. [Sir Norman Chester, *The Nationalisation of British Industry 1945–51* (London: HMSO, 1975) p. 1036] No general directives were issued by the 1945 Labour Government and few have been issued since then; this should not, however, be taken to imply a lack of subsequent intervention by Governments of both persuasions.

In the previous chapter the public corporation was described as an attempt to balance Government control with managerial autonomy. It has proved an impossible balance to achieve. One continuing source of controversy has been the right of Parliament to satisfy itself that the industries were acting efficiently and in accordance with the national interest. The first manifestation took place in the early years of nationalisation, with a running debate on the eligibility of Parliamentary Questions on the performance of the industries. Some types of question had always been refused by Ministers: these included questions on the subordinate organisations of the corporations, salaries (except of Board members) and staff matters. All these questions concerned issues that Ministers regarded as the day-to-day administration of the industries. In 1948 the Speaker of the House made a ruling which endorsed this practice, although since then questions have been more wide-ranging.

A number of Parliamentary Debates on the industries have subsequently been held, the first in 1949. The main post-war initiative in Parliamentary control, however, was the creation of a Select Committee on Nationalised Industries in 1952. The Committee has published a whole series of reports on individual industries and issues of general concern; its more important reports have been answered by the Government in the form of the publication of a White Paper. Generally these reports have reflected the orthodox view that nationalised industries should operate as commercial bodies at arm's length from the Government.

Probably the most important report presented by the SCNI was the result of their deliberations on the subject of Ministerial control. This report came to the conclusion that there was a 'sense of confusion and a general lack of clarity about purposes, policies, methods and responsibilities'. [First Report of the SCNI Session 1967-8, *Ministerial Control of the Nationalised Industries* HC 371-1 (London: HMSO, 1968) para. 114] Their main remedy was the creation of a Ministry of Nationalised Industries. The new Minister's principal duties would have been the appointment of the members of all the Boards, the establishment of pricing and investment policies, the agreement of financial objectives, the approval of investment projects, the furthering of co-ordination between industries, the instigation of efficiency studies, and accounting to Parliament for all the industries' activities.

The case for the establishment of such a Ministry had been made several times before and several times since the SCNI report. It was explicitly rejected in the Government's reply, which was published as a White Paper, *Ministerial Control of the Nationalised Industries* Cmnd 4027 (London: HMSO, 1969). The Government's opposition came from a recognition that the distinction between efficiency in one industry and the wider public interest need not imply that they should be the responsibilities of two different Ministers. In any case, the White Paper argued, a distinction in principle did not necessarily lead to an easy separation in practice; attempted separation would lead to increased bureaucracy.

Another recommendation contained in the SCNI report which has also been widely canvassed is the case for an external efficiency audit. The Report proposed that the Ministry of Nationalised Industries should look at the industries' costs, efficiency and prices and:

> If the Ministry were anxious about any aspect of a Board's work or performance, their first approach should be to discuss the problem informally with the Board or their officers; next they might suggest that the Board seek the assistance of some outside expert or should encourage them to seek advice overseas where this appears to be desirable; and lastly they might carry out, through a unit of their own, special studies in conjunction with the Board's officers of the problems concerned.
>
> [Ibid., para. 913]

To a certain extent an external audit was already in existence. In 1967 the Government announced that all major nationalised industry price increases would be referred to the National Board for Prices and Incomes, which would consider the underlying justification for any increase and the extent to which costs could be reduced by increased efficiency. These references ceased with the abolition of the Board by the 1970 Conservative Government and no efficiency audits of this form were undertaken until the Carter Committee on the Post Office reported in 1977.

An alternative, or a supplement, to Parliamentary and Ministerial intervention in the affairs of the industries is the establishment of clear financial and economic rules for their operation. If the ambiguous objectives of the initial Acts could be clarified by a set of precise guidelines for financial management, the performance of the industries could be monitored and accountability ensured without the need for external interference. Two post-war attempts were made to put this theory into practice.

The first attempt was made in 1961 by a Conservative Government with the publication of the first general review of the control principles for nationalised industries. [White Paper, *The Financial and Economic Obligations of the Nationalised Industries*, Cmnd 1337 (London: HMSO, 1961)] The White Paper specified the 'break-even' objective as 'surpluses on Revenue Account should be at least sufficient to cover deficits on Revenue Account *over a five year period*'; it clarified the desired provision for depreciation; and it stated that if an industry was required to depart from normal commercial pricing procedure it would be open to them to demand a written statement from the Minister.

The 1961 White Paper led the way to the introduction of financial targets for the industries. They were justified by the argument that, although the industries had obligations of a national and noncommercial kind, they ought not to be regarded as social services absolved from economic and commercial justification. Financial targets did not prove a success in practice. They were insufficiently related to overall economic policy; they were insufficiently flexible. Once set they were not altered in the light of changing economic circumstances. In 1967, when a new fuel policy was established, for example, the five-year objective set for the Gas Corporation was extended for a further two years at the previous level. The 1976 NEDO study already quoted summarised the effect of financial targetry in the following terms:

The Post Office's Telecommunications business, the Electricity Industry (England and Wales) and British Gas came near to achieving their targets throughout the 1960s but from 1971/2 onwards fell increasingly short as a result of Government price restraints. Targets were allowed to lapse in recognition of these exceptional circumstances. In the case of British Airways a three year target of a 7% return on net assets was established in 1972 – 6.5% was achieved – but was not renewed for 1975/6 despite the

Socialising Public Ownership

fact that statutory price restraints in the UK have relatively small impact in this case. No target was established for BSC until 1973 when a four year target of 8% on net assets was set and still remains in force. Although BSC's results were approximately in line with target after two years, the outturn for 1975/6 seems likely to make its achievement over four years impossible.

Any targets established for British Rail and NCB have tended to become rapidly obsolete in the light of actual outturns.

[*A Study of UK Nationalised Industries: Background Paper 1* (London: NEDO, 1976) p. 2]

A more important attempt to establish control rules was made by a Labour Government in 1967 [White Paper, *Nationalised Industries: A review of Economic and Financial Objectives*, Cmnd 3437 (London: HMSO, 1967)]. The precedence of 'economic' over 'financial', a reversal of the 1961 order, was deliberate; the White Paper contained guidance on investment and pricing policy which was designed to give the best allocation of national economic resources.

According to the White Paper, it was important that pricing policies should be devised with reference to the costs of the particular goods and services provided; in this way cross-subsidisation and misallocation of resources would be avoided. Prices should generally be related to the long-run costs at the margin, the cost of supplying an extra unit or service in the long run. This rule has its basis in welfare economics: it can be shown that overall satisfaction will be increased if prices are set equal to long-run costs for every good in every market.

It is difficult to say how successful marginal cost pricing could have been. Since, in economic theory at least, privately owned firms price their goods to profit-maximise, the idealised conceptions of welfare economics could not apply. It is also by no means certain whether the industries had the information available to introduce marginal cost pricing – another manifestation of the gap between theory and practice. In 1976 Coopers and Lybrand Associates were retained by NEDO to investigate the pricing policies in the British Gas Corporation, British Railways Board, British Steel Corporation and the Post Office. They concluded that none of the four industries based their prices policies on long-run or short-run marginal costs.

In part this was due to the operation of pure commercial considerations. In the main, however, the failure of marginal cost-pricing reflects one of the contradictory expectations: the nationalised industries were subsequently expected to act as instruments of resource allocation in a mixed economy and as the key element in the 1970 Conservative Government's anti-inflation policy. The second consideration rapidly became paramount and the attempts to apply financial discipline collapsed as a consequence.

Another new area of guidance contained in the 1967 White Paper was the endorsement of the Discounted Cash Flow technique as a method of investment appraisal. This too was an attempt to obtain the best balance of resources throughout the economy, but to achieve this objective the technique would have to be used generally in private industry – there has never been any evidence to demonstrate this. The Coopers and Lybrand study found that the technique was used in the four nationalised industries investigated, but that by its nature it could only be applied to a small percentage of the investment projects undertaken.

The White Paper also accepted a principle for controlling the industries that had been widely supported since the publication of the *Report of the Committee on the Electricity Supply Industry* in 1956. This was the view that the industries should concern themselves with commercial considerations, and social responsibilities were a matter for the Government. The Select Committee on Nationalised Industries had endorsed this idea in its report on Ministerial Control and suggested that when the Minister wished an industry to undertake a social obligation he should negotiate a separate contract. The 1967 White Paper recommended separate accounting for social responsibilities and the use of cost-benefit analysis techniques.

The conclusion must be that none of the attempts to introduce financial and economic control rules for the industries has been successful – though the ideas advanced in 1967 were never given a fair trial. The development of operational rules has never been accompanied by changes in the organisational structure of the public industrial sector. With the important exception of the operation of the National Enterprise Board in 1975 the changes have been peripheral. A new experimental way of financing the industries was introduced in the late 1960s for British Airways and the British Steel Corporation and it will be continued for the Aerospace and Shipbuilding Corporations. This experiment involved the creation of public dividend capital. Unlike loan stock, no predetermined rate of interest is paid on this form of finance; as in the case of private equity capital the level of payment, if any, is decided when the overall profit and loss is known. The Petroleum and Submarine Pipe-lines Act, which created the British National Oil Corporation, made the need to consult with the Government and trade unions more specific. It also laid down a statutory requirement that civil servants should be appointed to the Board, which represented a clear departure from previous practice. No other major new initiatives have been attempted and in a Parliamentary Debate held on 23 May 1975 a Government Minister was able to conclude by saying that the Government considered a good relationship with the industries to be 'arms length but not hands off'.

One major post-war organisational change amounted to a complete endorsement of the orthodox public corporation. In October 1969 the Post Office became a public corporation. The White Paper setting out the reasons for this change argued:

> The Government have carried out a fundamental review of the Post Office, set out against the challenging future of change and expansion which faces many of its services. Its present structure and methods are those of a Department of State. . . . A public corporation should be created to run these great businesses with a structure and methods designed directly to meet their needs drawing on best modern practice.
>
> [White Paper, *Reorganisation of the Post Office*, Cmnd 3233 (London: HMSO, 1967) para. 3]

These minor organisational changes to the public corporation structure and the new operational rules which have been introduced bear precious little relationship to the sentiments articulated by the ideological supporters of public ownership. None of the changes made since 1945 could be called socialist and inevitably the form of nationalisation adopted has disappointed its advocates. Many of them have been particularly dismayed at the failure to achieve co-ordination policies between the industries. This is worth considering in some detail because it shows how orthodox socialism has failed to get to grips with the problem of organisation in an advanced society.

The two sectors where there is an obvious case for co-ordination are energy and transport; in neither sector is public ownership complete, but since 1945 it has been extensive. Co-ordination between industries was a central argument in the Labour Party's case for nationalisation in 1945: the Party's manifesto had stated that co-ordination of transport could not be achieved without unification, and unification without public ownership would mean a struggle with sectional interests. At the heart of this argument was the view that efficient operation could be ensured by allocating resources within a sector as a whole, rather than within individual industries in the sector – thus, in the vocabulary of the time, eliminating wasteful competition. The interaction between industries was recognised much earlier in transport than in fuel, and there was also a long history of intervention in the railways.

The Coal Industry Nationalisation Act 1946, the Electricity Act 1947, the Transport Act 1947 and the Gas Act 1948 gave the Government extensive ownership in the fuel and transport industries. The Minister of Fuel and Power was given the responsibility of the co-ordination of energy policy, but a British Transport Commission was created to implement transport policy.

Under the 1947 Transport Act docks and inland waterways, hotels, railways, London Transport, road haulage and road passenger transport were administered by six Executive Boards. Overall responsibility was vested in the BTC, which had the general duty 'to exercise their powers under this Act to provide, or secure, or promote the provision of an efficient, adequate, economical and properly integrated system of public inland transport . . .'. The Commissioners were given a great deal of discretion to prepare the schemes of co-ordination and were offered little more than pious hopes from the Government. The task was beyond them.

The Commissioners were unable to cope with the volume of work which flowed from the task they were set. Before any effective policies could be implemented, it was essential that the individual industries were modernised and this called for a complex administrative task. As many as 4 per cent of the national labour force were at one time employed in BTC undertakings, and the problems of reorganisation were enormous. In the event, despite some local provision of joint services in rural areas, the individual industries continued to compete with each other.

The approach of the 1947 Act failed to take account of the sheer volume of bureaucratic decisions needed in a scheme of centralised co-ordination. The preparation of a Transport Charges Scheme provides a good example. The Commission was instructed to submit a statement of the principles on which charges for each of the transport services should be based and to submit this statement to a transport tribunal within two years. This timetable proved impossible to meet and it was subsequently extended for two further periods of two years. In the end the change in Government resulted in the abandonment of the scheme. Even if the scheme had been completed it would have needed immediate revision, as transport technology and demand were changing rapidly.

By 1951 it was apparent that the Transport Commissioners were making real but slow progress. However, the election of that year brought a Conservative Government to power which was determined to introduce a competitive decentralised structure. In 1952 they produced a White Paper which argued that little progress had been made and that 'even if integration in the fullest sense were practicable, it would result in a huge unwieldy machine, ill-adapted to meet with promptitude the varying and instant demands of industry'. [White Paper, *Transport Policy*, Cmd 8538 (London: HMSO, 1952) p. 2] Road haulage was partly denationalised, although resale of the vehicles was not as attractive as the Government hoped and the nationalised British Road Services remained the largest road haulage firm; the railways were encouraged to demonstrate inter-area rivalry.

The British Transport Commission became a holding company and was not formally dismantled until the 1962 Transport Act became law. This Act foreshadowed a reshaping of the network of passenger services and the new British Railways Board was given extensive freedom to compete for freight traffic. The railways had already run into recurring deficits and this continued despite the ensuing extensive programmes of passenger closures.

The reduction of the rail network proved politically unpopular and the 1964 Labour Party election manifesto attacked the reshaping programme and contained an explicit commitment to a national plan for co-ordinating transport. The 1964–70 Labour Government produced six separate White Papers on transport and in its 1968 Transport Act put on the statute book a most complex set of provisions designed to promote co-ordination and integration.

The 1968 Act contained three separate elements designed to promote the integration of freight: quantity licensing, the creation of a National Freight Corporation, and the establishment of a Freight Integration Council. Of these elements, quantity licensing was the most powerful and contentious: authorisation for the transport of certain types of road traffic would only be issued by a licensing authority if neither British Rail nor the NFC felt that the goods should be carried by rail.

In fact, quantity licensing was never implemented. The National Freight Corporation took over the road haulage interests held by the Transport Holding Company (the successor to the BTC) and the British Railways Board with a view to providing an integrated service. A separate Freightliner Company was established as a subsidiary to the NFC but with the Railways Board continuing to have a substantial financial interest; the Freightliner Company was instructed to send freight by rail whenever it was economic. The Freight Integration Council was an overall advisory body to consider co-ordination between all the nationalised industries including the Post Office and the airlines.

The call for the integration of freight is frequently a synonym for the transfer of goods from road to rail. This is an attractive idea: the railway network is already in existence, it is used well below its capacity and has always been attractive to environmentalists. Judged by this criterion the success of the 1968 Act has been limited. The NFC has overseen a shift away from rail towards road traffic; there has been a concerted campaign by the Rail Board and the unions for the return of Freightliners to them; the Freight Integration Council has had no impact.

The most important shortcoming of the 1968 Act, however, concerned the failure to place railway finances on a sound footing. Grants for socially necessary, but unprofitable, railway services were introduced by the Act and there was a reduction in railway capital debt. Profits were earned in the years immediately following the Act; but thereafter a financial deterioration set in, and this led eventually to the Railways Act of 1974, which replaced separate grants by a global subsidy for the whole passenger network. In 1974 the Government made provision for £1500 million of subsidies for the following five years, but by the following year it was clear that this sum would be totally inadequate.

The most recent approach to transport policy has been far more tentative. In 1976 the Government published a two-volume consultative document and invited interested parties to contribute before a White Paper was produced. [*Transport Policy: A Consultation Document* (London: HMSO, 1976] The document's stated intention was to set out the main policy options, but it implicitly rejected an approach based on centralised management. Instead, the task for Government was to be the establishment of the correct framework in which individual choice could be exercised. The establishment of a National Authority to organise inland transport was rejected; an advisory National Transport Council was offered in its place. The White Paper was published in the following year and endorsed the policy set out in the consultative document. No National Transport Council is to be created and the role of the Government is to provide a 'rational and realistic framework' for fair competition. [White Paper, *Transport Policy,* Cmnd 6836 (London: HMSO, 1977]

All of this is a far cry from the demands made by Labour Party activists. A most fitting epitaph to post-war transport policy was made by the President of the Transport Salaried Staffs Association, Tom Bradley, MP, in his reply to the transport debate at the 1975 Annual Conference, when he said, 'Conference, meeting here in 1949, would have found it unbelievable if someone had forecast then that a quarter of a century later we would still be debating the case for and the need for a properly integrated system of public transport. Yet that is the position.' [LPACR (Blackpool), 1975, p. 277]

An integrated fuel policy has never had the same appeal as an integrated transport policy. Most of the energy produced is used by industry rather than domestic consumers and the problems of the fuel industries tend to be technical rather than organisational. These factors account for the lesser public interest. There have only been two post-war White Papers which were statements of fuel policy in the sense that they went beyond a consideration of the needs of one industry.

The period since 1945 has seen a marked change in the fortunes of the coal industry. A decade of excess demand was followed, with a reduction in the relative price of oil, by a sharp contraction in the market; the dramatic increase in oil prices that occurred after the 1973 war in the Middle East led to a complete reversal of policy and an attempt to reinvest and increase the potential coal supply. The discovery of offshore reserves of oil and gas and the growth of nuclear power have both had enormous impacts on the supply and demand of inland energy.

Successive governments have, however, chosen to manage these changing circumstances without resorting to the institutional approach that has categorised transport policy. A 1952 Committee on National Policy for the Use of Fuel and Power Resources (the Ridley Committee) concluded that the best use of resources would result if consumers had free choice between fuels and the market system was allowed to operate. This was the characteristic approach until the coal industry ran into problems caused by falling demand in the late 1950s. A first measure of protection was introduced in 1961 with a tax on fuel oil of 2d a gallon.

The first White Paper [*Fuel Policy*, Cmnd 2798 (London: HMSO, 1965)] was produced to discuss the implication of the estimates of energy requirements set out in the National Plan. A continuing rundown in the coal industry was projected and a capital reconstruction of the industry was implemented as a consequence. The second White Paper followed only two years later [*Fuel Policy*, Cmnd 3438 (London: HMSO, 1967)] and took account of the development of cheap North Sea gas. The White Paper boldly announced that the nation was moving from a two-fuel to a four-fuel economy.

A series of measures to ease the transition in the coal industry were implemented. The most contentious has been the use of the electricity industry to stabilise the demand for coal. The Central Electricity Generating Board has consistently opposed this policy and resented being 'used as pawns in the game to tie up the loose ends of the country's energy strategy'. [Sir Arthur Hawkins, Chairman of the CEGB, speaking at the National Energy Conference, 22 June 1976]

A new development in the formulation of energy policy with wide implications for the control of public ownership, took place immediately following the election of a Labour Government in 1974. In the aftermath of the oil price increases and the miners' strike the new Government decided to establish a Coal Industry Examination Committee 'to consider and advise on the contribution which coal can best make to the country's energy requirements and the steps needed to secure that contribution'. What was significant was the establishment of the Committee on a tripartite basis, with representatives of the Government, the Coal Board and the mining trade unions. This experiment marked the most important advance of the trade union movement into policy formulation.

Given the composition of the Committee, it was hardly surprising that it endorsed the NCB's expansionist *Plan for Coal*. Nevertheless, the success of the approach prompted the Government to create a permanent Energy Commission, an advisory body with representatives from the energy industries and trade unions. Taken together with the transport consultation document, these developments in energy policy demonstrate a much more tentative attitude towards the formulation of sector policy. The Government appears to be far more ready to recognise potential contradictions and negotiate a compromise in advance, and much less ready to transfer the whole problem to an institution for solution.

This review of the failure of sector policy to meet expectations, and the previous discussion on the organisation and operating rules of the nationalised industries, show that the implementation of public ownership has continually been a problem area in modern socialism. The view that it has received insufficient attention in the Labour Party has already been advanced. In the absence of a clear Government policy the nationalised industries have simply carried on muddling through.

Muddling through leads eventually to a crisis; and the problems of the nationalised industries had reached these proportions when the 1974 Labour Government took office. The 1974/5 results underlined the disastrous effects of the earlier price restraint on financial accountability. The combined deficits of the industries were variously reported as exceeding £1000 million and the Post Office's deficit of £304 million was described as the world's biggest-ever loss. A dispute between the Government and Board members on the level of the latter's pay was developing in intensity. In June 1975 the Government announced, in a White Paper reply to the Select Committee, that it had asked the National Economic Development Office to undertake an inquiry into the role of nationalised industries in the economy and the way in which they are to be controlled in future.

A *Times* editorial of the following month summarised the problems of the industries at the time as:

> Each state enterprise is different, yet what is common is the atmosphere of crisis. It has already driven the various Chairmen to band together and to send a deputation to Downing Street to plead for a new deal. To be a Chairman or a Board Member in the public sector is to invite vilification. The customers are openly antagonistic. Governments constantly interfere in decision taking and always believe they know better, while nationalised industries' management is not noted for enjoying high levels of their employees' confidence. Nor are those who carry the can for losses, not always of their making, paid a particularly attractive rate for the scapegoat's job. [*The Times*, 24 July 1975]

The NEDO Study covered almost the same ground as the 1967–8 SCNI investigation, although it restricted detailed investigations to the nine major corporations, which employed more than 50,000 people. The main part of the study was published in November 1976, and its conclusion suggested that the sentiments expressed by The *Times* leader could not be dismissed as the overstatement of a hostile correspondent. Although recognising that generalisations were difficult the NEDO report was categorical in its denunciation of the current arrangements:

> Nevertheless, there are certain features of the relationship be-
> tween Government and nationalised industries which came
> through so clearly in our inquiry that we believe they can be
> stated without risk of contradiction:
>   there is a lack of trust and mutual understanding between those
> who run the nationalised industries and those in Government
> (politicians and civil servants) who are concerned in their affairs;
>   there is confusion about the respective roles of the Boards of
> nationalised industries, Ministers and Parliament, with the result
> that accountability is seriously blurred;
>   there is no systematic framework for reaching agreement on
> long-term objectives and strategy, and no assurance of continuity
> when decisions are reached;
>   there is no effective system for measuring the performance of
> nationalised industries and assessing managerial competence.
>   [*A Study of UK Nationalised Industries*
>   (London: NEDO, 1976) p. 8]

The NEDO Study contained the most detailed analysis of these underlying problems and proposed some useful recommendations for resolving them. Unfortunately the discussion of its findings was dominated by a general antipathy towards one of its main sugges-tions: the creation of a Policy Council for each major industry. The Policy Council's main function would be to agree corporate objec-tives and strategies, endorse corporate plans, and monitor perform-ance. Underneath the Council would be a Corporation Board which would manage the corporation within the agreed framework. What was particularly controversial was the suggestion that the Policy Council should include members of the Corporation Board, civil servants, trade unionists and 'members reflecting users' and other independent viewpoints'.

Acceptance of this proposal would have marked the end of the acceptance of 'arm's length' management of the corporations. It reflected a view that intervention was inevitable and should be institutionalised. The one industry Chairman who was a member of NEDO's advisory group, Nigel Foulkes of the British Airports

Authority, justified it in the following terms: 'The Policy Council brings into the same room representatives of the Civil Service, the unions, the Corporation Board, and independents, and invites them to use their power and knowledge as a continuous, visible, and accountable process of decision-making by the "stake-holders".' [Letter to *The Times,* 23 November 1976] The Policy Council idea, however, was rejected by most of the Chairmen and trade union leaders.

One source of NEDO's justification for formalising intervention was its consideration of public enterprise in France, Germany and Sweden. The term 'public enterprise' was used in the study to denote the fact that many of the public-sector activities considered were not created or controlled by an Act of nationalisation. In France a system of control has evolved where the industries are integrated into the system of national planning: the Ministers are extensively represented within the industries, and this involvement has worked successfully. In Germany a new form of organisation has emerged: a departmental agency, which has no separate legal personality but has a separate identity for trading purposes. The extent of public enterprise in Sweden is less than in the other two countries, but a well-developed State Holding Company (Statsforetag AB) and an audit bureau (Riksrevisionsverket) exist.

The NEDO Study suggested that these continental methods of control worked a great deal better than the British experience:

> Relations between the enterprises and the Ministries are good, the control operates smoothly and neither from those concerned with the control nor from Parliament or the press are there any proposals for major changes in the system. There is thus a conspicuous difference in attitudes between the UK and three Continental countries. [*Background Paper 2,* p. 28]

The relative success abroad was ascribed to maintaining a distinction between enterprises operating in a competitive environment and those which are monopolies or quasi-monopolies. For the latter, Government intervention is accepted:

> In the case of enterprises not in the competitive sector, there is acceptance of the primacy of public policy over commercial autonomy, even on such matters as prices and the level of services. *Prima facie* this had no effect on efficiency and initiative. Where Ministers have more discretion, there is tighter financial control by Parliament, in Sweden particularly. All three countries have an institution engaged in effectiveness auditing of public enterprises to a greater or lesser extent; but there is little criticism of the enterprises' efficiency. . . . [Ibid., p. 33]

The Government promised to respond to the NEDO ideas with a White Paper on the role of nationalised industries. The publication of this Paper has been delayed by underlying differences of emphasis between the different Government Departments. When it is published it is likely to contain an endorsement of the 'arms length' view of the control of public corporations, while drawing on the lessons of post-war years. A framework of financial targets will probably be introduced, supplemented by broader performance criteria. The Price Commission could be asked to act as an efficiency auditor. Representation on Boards will be broadened, but the universal introduction of Policy Councils rejected. Finally, it seems likely that the power of Ministerial direction will be regularised.

A consideration of public ownership since the war must, however, point to the need for more radical change. Piecemeal reforms have not proved successful and the form of organisation must be considered as well as the mode of operation. Such a thorough-going review is now, in any case, prompted by the growing demands for greater industrial democracy which can no longer be brushed aside. This chapter has concentrated on the economic problems of industrial public ownership; the role of the workers will be examined in the next.

Chronology

1926   The Central Electricity Board established by the *Electricity (Supply) Act* to regulate the central generation of electricity.

1933   The London Passenger Transport Board established.

1946   *Civil Aviation Act* creates British European Airways and British South American Airways. British Overseas Airways Corporation, which had been established in 1939, included in the consequent reorganisation.

1947   National Coal Board, created by *Coal Industry Nationalisation Act 1946*, begins operations.

1948   Overall responsibility for transport co-ordination placed in hands of the British Transport Commission established by the *Transport Act 1947*. Railways Executive, Road Passenger Transport Executive, Road Haulage Executive, London Transport Executive, Docks, Harbours and Inland Waterways Executive and the Hotels Executive all placed under the umbrella of BTC.

1948   British Electricity Authority, created by the *Electricity Act 1947*, begins operations.

1949   Gas Council and twelve Area Gas Boards, created by the *Gas Act 1948*, begin operations.

1949   *Iron and Steel Act* passed, creating Iron and Steel Corporation of Great Britain, with vesting day in 1951.

1952   'Ridley Committee' on *The Use of Fuel and Power Resources* supports free market in energy.
         Select Committee on Nationalised Industries established.

1953   Steel industry denationalised by *Iron and Steel Act 1953*, which creates Iron and Steel Board.
         Transport Act denationalises some road haulage and reduces BTC to role of Holding Company.

1961   White Paper, *The Financial and Economic Obligations of the Nationalised Industries* (Cmnd 1337), specifies break-even period as five years and leads to the introduction of financial targets.

1962   *Transport Act* replaces BTC by Transport Holding Company and provides for the establishment of separate Boards for Railways, London Transport, Docks and Waterways.

1965 and 1967   *Fuel Policy* White Papers (Cmnd 2798 and 3438) accept gradual contraction of coal industry and recommend measures to ease transition.

1967   Major parts of steel industry renationalised by *Iron and Steel Act*.
         White Paper, *Nationalised Industries: A Review of Economic and Financial Objectives* (Cmnd 3437), recommends

use of marginal cost pricing and discounted cash flow techniques.

1968   SCNI report, *Ministerial Control of the Nationalised Industries,* recommends establishment of a Ministry of Nationalised Industry – subsequently rejected by Government.
Transport Act sets out a complex series of measures designed to promote transport integration at local and national levels. National Freight Corporation created.

1969   Post Office becomes a public corporation.

1970   Conservative Government announces decision to hive off some profitable ancillaries of nationalised industries.

1971   *Rolls-Royce* (1971) added to public sector following collapse as private company.

1974   *Coal Industry Examination Committee* established on a tripartite basis with representatives of Government, unions and management.

1975   *Petroleum and Submarine Pipe-lines Act* creates BNOC.
Industry Act creates National Enterprise Board.

1976   Consultation document on *Transport Policy* published, rejects approach based on centralised management.
National Economic Development Office publishes *A Study of UK Nationalised Industries* which suggests establishment of Policy Council for the major industries.
British Aerospace and British Shipbuilders established by *Aircraft and Shipbuilding Act.*

1977   *Transport Policy* White Paper (Cmnd 6836) rejects idea of National Transport Council to co-ordinate policy.

3 The Role of the Workers

Public ownership makes possible a great extension of the part that workers can play in the running of the industries in which they are employed. At the same time, by removing the element of private profit and by making management responsible to the community instead of to private shareholders, public ownership should reduce sources of conflict and promote a better spirit within the industries concerned.

[TUC, *Public Ownership: An Interim Report 1953*]

'Socialisation' implies that nationalisation should amount to more than simply a change in the ownership of an industry. One aspect of socialisation has historically commanded universal support within the Labour Movement: the notion that public ownership should act to the benefit of the workers in the industry. Unfortunately it in this aspect of the performance of publicly-owned industry that has caused the biggest disappointment to its ideological advocates. Although no supporter of nationalisation would argue that the public corporations have been worse employers than their counterparts in the private sector, most would agree that the transformation in the relationship between man and management that had been expected has not taken place.

A consideration of the comparative failure in the field of industrial relations must start from a recognition of two basic facts. The first is that demands for a greater role for the workers in the industries have been made by advocates who held very different views about what that role should be – the most important division being the supporters and opponents of workers' control. The second is that the case for increasing the power of the workforce has been argued for privately owned as well as publicly owned industry. Public ownership, it is true, gives the state the power to alter the internal organisation of the industry concerned without facing the opposition of shareholders – this has been the basis of an important historic argument for nationalisation. In practice many of the problems involved in increasing worker power apply equally to public and private sectors.

Arguments for an enhanced status for workers tend to stem from a similar political sentiment: that a movement away from 'wage-slavery' towards a greater say in the control of industry gives dignity to labour. The most frequently quoted early statement of this case is the evidence that William Straker, Secretary of the Northumberland Miners' Association, gave to the Sankey Commission on the Coal Industry in 1919:

In deciding what is to be the character of mines administration
it is necessary to remember that workmen are more than machines
or even 'hands' as they are so often termed. Industrial unrest is
a question about which everyone is concerned, yet there is a
general lack of appreciation of what is the real root of this unrest. . . . The fact is that the unrest is deeper than can be reached
by merely pounds, shillings and pence necessary as these are.
The root of the matter is the straining of the spirit of man to be
free. Once he secures the freedom of the spirit he will, as a natural
sequence, secure a material welfare equal to what united brains
and hands can wring from mother earth and her surrounding
atmosphere. Any administration of the mines, under nationalisation, must not leave the mine worker in the position of a mere
wage-earner, whose sole energies are directed by the will of another. He must have a share of the management of the industry
in which he is engaged, and understand all about the purpose
and destination of the product he is producing; he must know
both the productive and the commercial side of the industry.

> [*Coal Industry Commission: Minutes of Evidence,*
> Cmd 359 (London: HMSO, 1919) p. 324]

Straker's plea for a greater share in the management of the industry
for the workers has been echoed, though less eloquently, ever since;
but there has been continuing disagreement over the form that the
share in management should take. Two radically different, though
superficially similar, views were expressed by socialists to the Sankey
Commission. Sidney Webb, in his evidence, supported a scheme for
the formation of Pit Committees composed of managerial officials
and employee representatives which would offer counsel and criticism [ibid., p. 482]. G. D. H. Cole put the case for 'the establishment at once of the greatest amount of industrial democracy (that
is, of direct control by the workers and their trade unions) that is
immediately practicable, and the most rapid extension of that control that is practicable subsequently' [ibid., p. 549]. Webb's opposition to workers' control, which had led to the compromise over the
Labour Party's Constitution, has already been noted; Cole was, by
this time, an advocate of the doctrine. Their differences were fundamental.

This chapter is mainly concerned with the performance of the
nationalised industries since 1945 and the growing demands for
much greater worker participation in management. Some background discussion on the philosophies that were held by advocates
and opponents of workers' control will, however, enable the post-
war experience to be put into an historical context.

'Workers' control' is traditionally associated in Britain with two
distinct political viewpoints: syndicalism and guild socialism.

Syndicalism was an important force in the trade unions before 1914 and the British movement owes a great deal to French inspiration. Syndicalists proposed the trade union as the mechanism for government; self-governing workshops would provide representatives who would replace legislators elected from geographical constituencies. Its supporters believed that this form of society could only be achieved by revolutionary action on the part of trade unions. Guild socialism had its roots far more firmly in British experience and was based on a recognition of the responsibility that workers' control places on organised labour. Guild socialists argued that the trade unions must become national guilds and include all workers in an industry as members. Supporters of the national guilds, G. D. H. Cole among them, suggested a form of nationalisation which would involve the devolution of power to the representatives chosen from amongst the guildsmen.

At the time that the Guilds Movement was growing in importance, greater consultation was widely advocated as an alternative to workers' control. The Whitley Committee on Relations between Employers and Employed had issued five reports between 1917 and 1918: their conclusions were that the State should set up joint management–employee committees where workers could be consulted on production and related welfare matters. Many 'Whitley Councils' were set up, but most became bargaining bodies and the broader consultative aspects were ignored. Eventually the success of Joint Production Committees in the Second World War provided a climate of opinion in the trade union movement which was favourable to an approach based on joint consultation.

The first chapter of this book outlined the argument on worker representation in nationalised industries which reached a climax in the early 1930s when Herbert Morrison faced his opponents at successive TUC and Labour Conferences. The eventual victory of the supporters of consultation rather than control was described. By 1945 joint consultation was seen as the major gain in industrial relations that would be secured by nationalisation.

Each of the industries that was nationalised after the war was placed under a statutory obligation to create two separate types of machinery: one for the negotiation of wages and conditions of service and another for joint consultation. Consultative machinery was established to provide management with advice and to give employees a sense of participation. Management's sole right to take decisions remained; joint consultative committees were to be advisory as distinct from executive. All the industries were instructed to consult with recognised unions on matters of safety, health, welfare and all matters of common interest to the Boards and their employees. The machinery created varied from industry to industry. All committees were composed of representatives of management and unions; every industry had national, regional and local levels; there were, however, wide differences in functions and even the terminology varied. The most important distinction occurred between those industries where joint consultation was kept separate from negotiation and those where the same committee undertook both functions – though at different times.

Perhaps the most complex machinery was established in the coal industry. The coal industry is almost unique, for a satisfactory relationship between management and unions is a precondition for any production, let alone profitability. Because of the ever-present threat from hostile geology, combined action is essential. A brief outline of the arrangement established in the National Coal Board is, however worth while for two reasons. Mining was where the greatest improvement in industrial relations was expected and a consideration of the procedures introduced illustrates a major difficulty which underlies all joint consultation arrangements.

National, Divisional and Area Consultative Committees were charged with the consideration and recommendation of matters concerned with safety, health, welfare and the organisation and conduct of operations. These committees all met monthly. A consultative committee was also established at each of the 950 collieries: its function included the review of accident and sickness trends, training and educational facilities, weekly output performance, current and future development plans, and technical reports by the colliery manager.

It is too easy, with hindsight, to underestimate the very real victory that the trade unions thought they had won when joint consultation was accepted. Frank Smith, Secretary-Agent of the Leicestershire National Union of Mineworkers from 1945 to 1976, expressed his views on the creation of consultative committees in the following terms: 'Joint consultation was new, fresh, and was the way for the union to participate and make a contribution to the industry. In their official capacity the NUM representatives now had the constitutional right to meet management at area and divisional level and a legal right to voice their opinions' [from an interview with the author]. Frank Smith could not recall an occasion when the alternative of workers' control was seriously discussed in the period prior to nationalisation.

In retrospect, with such high expectations for the system, the disillusionment that followed was inevitable. Joint consultation in the coal industry had no chance of achieving the high hopes of its advocates – and this was true of all the public corporations. By 1949 the TUC had accepted a resolution calling for greater workers' participation in the nationalised industries; the General Council undertook a survey of consultation which attributed the difficulties to lack of experience on both sides. Three years later a further resolution led to another TUC survey and a number of problems were identified. Dissatisfaction with joint consultation was said to be due to the following factors: the lingering demand for workers' control; a failure to accept that joint consultation was advisory and not executive; a failure of management to adjust their attitudes; overcentralisation of the structure itself. The overall conclusion of the TUC survey was still favourable and the report concluded 'that experience of joint consultation in the nationalised industry has not revealed any fundamental weakness calling for a radical change in Congress policy'. [*Public Ownership: An Interim Report* (London: TUC, 1953) p. 24]

An earlier study of joint consultation undertaken by the Acton Society Trust in the previous year had arrived at similar conclusions. Key problems in the operation of joint consultation were identified as too much centralisation, defects in the basis of representation, and a failure to apply the spirit of consultation. Centralisation was a problem because too many matters raised at the local level were referred to higher levels and several months elapsed before they were settled. Problems of representation occurred because certain unions were squeezed out of consultation. This criticism applies to the present day: the Association of Professional, Executive, Clerical and Computer Staff (APEX), with 5300 members in the coal industry, is not represented on the National Consultative Committee. The failure to apply the spirit of consultation was the most fundamental defect. The Acton study suggested that all too often the advisory character of the committees degenerated into confrontation.

The comparative failure of joint consultation was seen to result from expectations which were too high:

Many of the hopes placed on joint consultation were highly unrealistic, a situation which no conceivable modification of the machinery can remedy. On the employees' side, there were too many who attributed every inconvenience to the unreasonableness of management and who believed that when joint consultation was introduced their complaints would be rectified. Now that events have shown that improvement is more difficult than they supposed, they tend, too easily, to become impatient and to lose interest. Those who visualised joint consultation as a step towards workers' control are even more impatient. On the employers' side, while there were many who put no faith in joint consultation, there were others who expected it to promote a new enthusiasm and interest in efficiency, as well as making for a more co-operative attitude on the part of the unions: to a large extent, these hopes have also been disappointed. Not only were these hopes too optimistic in themselves, but to some extent they were inconsistent.

[*Nationalised Industry: The Framework of Joint Consultation*
(London: Acton Society, 1952) p. 22]

Overambitious hopes, overcentralisation and a failure to operate
the machinery available all contributed to the comparative failure
of joint consultation. However, the benefit of thirty years' hindsight
points to a more fundamental problem. Joint consultation failed to
recognise the essential bargaining relationship that underlies all
contact between management and unions – and this relationship
is far more pronounced in the British than the continental tradition of trade unionism. It is arguable that 'co-operation and working together' is only really possible when it emerges from that bargaining framework.

Certainly amongst trade unions since the war there has been a
growing rejection of the idea that some issues are negotiable and
others only the subject of consultation. The development of this
view, and a recognition of the importance of the bargaining framework, underlies much of today's debate about the best form of industrial democracy for public ownership. This debate, which did
not really develop until the middle of the 1960s, will be discussed
at length later in this chapter. Before doing so a digression is necessary.

It would be wrong to regard participation in management as the
only issue at stake in securing an improvement in the dignity of
labour. Historically, the elimination of the profit motive from the
management of industry was suggested at various times as likely to
lead to a more democratic system of management appointments,
improved wages, better opportunities for trade unions to organise,
and less likelihood of redundancy.

The system of Board appointments, the list of 'the Great and the
Good', has come in for some deserved criticism, but below this level
an improved system of managerial appointments has taken place.
The objective assessment of candidates at promotion boards, taking
place under structures agreed with the appropriate trade unions, is
standard practice – there is no evidence of nepotism. Morrison had
argued that the industries must become Napoleonic armies with
promotions from the ranks; he would be satisfied with what has
been achieved. In this respect, as in many others, the nationalised
industries have proved far better employers than the private sector.
The critical discussion of joint consultation and the analysis which
follows must be seen against this background. Sick pay, pension
schemes and other conditions of employment have also been well in
advance of provisions elsewhere.

There has been no evidence, on the other hand, that wages in
the nationalised industries have shown a marked increase above

trend. The 1976 NEDO study considered movements in wages over the period 1960–75 and concluded that the earnings of manual workers in the major public corporations increased slightly less than other sectors in the 1960s, but since 1970 the reverse is true. The relative improvement in recent years is mainly due to pay increases in the coal industry. Nationalised industries have tended to feel the impact of Government incomes policies rather more than industry as a whole, partly because wage bargaining is undertaken on a national basis, but mainly because of Government insistence on rigid compliance with voluntary policies.

The 1970s have also witnessed a number of important wage disputes which resulted from the opposition of trade unions in nationalised industries to the prevailing Government policy. These disputes, particularly the Post Office dispute of 1971 and the miners' strikes of 1972 and 1974, took the form of a confrontation between the trade union movement and the Conservative Government. These large strikes have distorted the number of days lost through disputes in the major public corporations which, by comparison with private industry, would otherwise appear relatively strike-free. From an orthodox trade union point of view, the industrial relations system in the major public corporations has been good: unions have been recognised, given extensive bargaining facilities, and, most recently, there has been wide acceptance of the introduction of closed shop agreements for compulsory union membership.

There is one area where the success of the industrial relations practice has been most evident and in the light of the historic arguments for nationalisation this success is ironic. The decline in manpower that has taken place in most of the public corporations has been handled with surprisingly little friction. Despite the hopes of guaranteed employment under nationalisation the industries have faced an inevitable and continuing decline in employment. In the National Coal Board employment fell by 56 per cent between 1960 and 1975; in 1968 alone 64,000 jobs were lost. A rundown of a similar scale has taken place in British Rail. Both industries have achieved considerable success in avoiding the worst impact of redundancies by a combination of natural wastage and, particularly in the coal industry, moving potentially redundant employees elsewhere in the industry. The NEDO study concluded that major reorganisations have been handled with a minimum amount of industrial disruption and, in the context of this upheaval, the strike record of the nationalised industries is good:

It is unlikely that similar private industries could have achieved reductions in employment levels of this order without major industrial conflict which did not occur in the nationalised industries. Close consultation between management and unions has been instrumental in achieving reorganisation of many of the industries studied.

[*A Study of UK Nationalised Industries: Background Paper 4*
(London: NEDO, 1977) p. 2]

In recent years, however, the debate on the role of the workers in the publicly owned industries has concentrated almost exclusively on the issue of increased worker participation. The other areas of potential gain for the workers have been given much less consideration; it is arguable whether this concentration on participation, to the detriment of other considerations relating to the employment arrangements in the nationalised industries, has been correct and this will be considered later. In the remainder of this chapter the vocabulary of the debate will be outlined, the major European experience discussed and the recent domestic controversy considered.

'Industrial democracy' is now on the agenda everywhere. Legislation has been introduced, amended or considered in both developed and developing countries. Since its successful implementation would alter the power structure within industry it is a highly charged and emotive subject as the furore following the publication of the 1977 Bullock Report bears witness; the term industrial democracy itself can only be clearly defined in relation to the background political system where its introduction is under consideration.

The ambiguities surrounding the use of the term industrial democracy were thoroughly explored in the research reports prepared for the Bullock Committee:

A strict usage of the term would indicate the ability of workers to change the 'government' in industry or to determine directly management decisions. In practice, 'industrial democracy', along with a host of associated ideas, is often used to denote far more limited forms of influence and involvement, even including the receipt of information and 'participative' styles of supervision.

[Eric Batstone, *Industrial Democracy and Worker Representation at Board Level* (London: HMSO, 1976) p. 10]

There are two dimensions to any system of worker participation: the extent to which it is intended to change the nature of decision-making and the mechanism which is chosen to achieve this purpose.

At its lowest level of ambition, worker participation is a management technique aimed at securing better methods of work organisation and improved communication. Management's prerogative to take decisions is left completely unchallenged. This view of worker participation is heavily paternalistic and is often accompanied by the view that managers are qualified by ability and experience to act in the best interests of the workforce anyway. The next level in participation consists of those methods where workers are represented on joint committees which have advisory but not executive powers; joint consultation provides a good example. More positive forms of participation are aimed at radically changing the power relationship between owner and employee and manager and managed. In the public sector the elimination of shareholders means that some alternatives which are relevant in privately owned firms, like profit-sharing schemes, need not be considered.

Once agreement has been reached on the extent to which the power of decision-making should be dispersed, a discussion must take place on the method of implementing the required change. Growing disenchantment with purely consultative mechanisms has led to increased interest in a number of alternatives; these include an extension of collective bargaining, joint decision-making, worker representatives on Boards, and self-management. Each of these alternatives has a different impact on the role of the trade union movement. A consideration of developments in Sweden, Germany and Yugoslavia shows the different emphases that have been given to these alternatives in different political systems.

In Sweden the main emphasis has been on securing participation through collective bargaining – the process leading to a collective agreement between employer and trade union. The 1976 Co-determination at Work Act sets out, in Article 32, the underlying philosophy:

> Between parties to a collective agreement on pay and general conditions of employment there should, if the union side so requests, also be concluded a collective agreement on co-determination for employees in questions relating to concluding and cancelling employment contracts, to supervision and distribution of work or to other aspects of management.

In 1972 Sweden began an experimental period of worker representation on Boards, and this was extended, four years later, to cover enterprises with as few as twenty-five employees. However, the unions looked to Board representation as an adjunct to collective bargaining: worker-directors were expected to provide the unions with greater information and knowledge.

The system that has attracted the most interest in Britain has been the West German system for worker representation on Boards and for co-determination in the coal and steel industries. West Germany has been the model for the two-tier Board system; German law requires the establishment of a Supervisory Board, whose members are nominated by both workers and shareholders, and a Managing Board, whose members are nominated by the Supervisory Board. The powers of the Supervisory Board are limited and to a large extent the arrangement legitimises management authority.

Workers in the German coal and steel industries have half the seats on a Supervisory Board which meets under a neutral chairman. Until recently workers in other public companies had a third of the seats. In 1976 co-determination was extended to all major companies and over the following two years the proportion of worker-directors must be increased to a half. Even so the shareholders would still be able, if they were determined, to preserve their ultimate authority: the chairman will be chosen by the Board but if the required two-thirds majority is not forthcoming it will be the shareholders' choice that prevails. Further, the new legislation stipulates that at least one of the worker representatives must come from the ranks of senior management. It is the West German pattern that has been recommended by the EEC. The Draft Statute for European Companies suggests that countries consider standardising their method of participation by introducing a two-tier system with one-third worker representatives on the Supervisory Board. The Draft Statute also recommends that all employees, whether trade union members or not, should be allowed a vote in the ballot for worker representatives.

The radical alternative to collective bargaining and co-determination is workers' control or self-management. Yugoslavia has provided the biggest source of inspiration to advocates of this philosophy. Industrial organisation in Yugoslavia differs in several important respects from the rest of Eastern Europe: there is a market economy with competition between firms organised on the principle that capital should work for labour and not vice–versa; each firm and each factory is responsible to the zbor or assembly of all the workers.

The director of the firm is elected by the workers from a shortlist agreed between the workers' council, itself elected by the workers, and the local administrative authority. Day-to-day problems are considered by a management committee, also composed of elected worker representatives and the director, though he has no vote. The Yugoslavian experiment in workers' control, though established over twenty-five years ago, is continually evolving.

The varying strands that have characterised the continental experience of industrial democracy have been reflected in the debate that has developed in Britain. The domestic debate has been confused: everyone has been at pains to stress heartfelt support for the abstract idea but the prescriptions offered have frequently been vague and contradictory. On occasions the looseness of the vocabulary of participation has been used to conceal fundamental differences of opinion.

The turning point in the debate in Britain came with the publication of the 1968 report of the *Royal Commission on Trade Unions and Employers' Associations*, Cmnd 3623 (the Donovan Commis-

sion). The report itself gave scant consideration to industrial democracy: only three and a half pages of the report discussed the problem and the Commission argued that the reform of collective bargaining would be the best way for workers to influence decisions
at their workplace. Of much more significance was the TUC's evidence, which represented a marked departure from its previously
held position.

The TUC recommended participation at three distinct levels.
At the plant level workers' representatives should sit on whatever
was the effective decision-making body; at intermediate levels the
workers should similarly be represented; at Board level companies
should allow union representation although the TUC recognised
that this would require a change in company law. The Commission
was opposed to the first two proposals and divided on the third.
Five members expressed qualified support for worker-directors.

In the previous year a Labour Party Working Party on Industrial
Democracy had reported. The document that it produced was
thoughtful and well argued and emphasised the importance of
basing any extension of participation firmly on the trade union
movement. The Working Party's report recognised that participation could be enhanced by a variety of methods and demonstrated
a clear preference for the extension of collective bargaining. On
worker-directors the report was tentative, calling for the need for
more experimentation.

Over the following five years the debate followed the guidelines
established by the TUC evidence and the Labour Party report.
There was universal recognition of the need for greater participation but a general reluctance to advocate one method of achieving
the desired result at the expense of the others. Worker-directors
were seen as a worthwhile experiment; collective bargaining was
the most frequently advocated method of increasing the influence
of the workforce at lower levels. Only systems which were based on
the existing trade union structure were thought likely to have any
impact.

A speech delivered by Harold Wilson in 1973, later published by
the Labour Party in pamphlet form as *Democracy in Industry*
(London: The Labour Party, 1973) shows just how exploratory
views on the subject were. Wilson argued that government by con-
sent needed to be extended to industry and that the decision-taking
process ought to be widened. His recommendations included the
extension of collective bargaining 'through trade union channels to
include joint decisions on work-routine, factory layout, work-load
arrangements, assembly line speeds and techniques as well as general
production methods', a compulsory system of works committees
'elected from the shop floor in elections organised and administered
by the trade unions' (it was not clear from his speech whether they

would be executive or merely advisory), and 'wider experimentation, on the lines begun by the Labour Government in steel, for placing representatives of the worker directly concerned on the relevant boards, including regional boards'. [pp. 12, 13]

Two groups had, by this time, developed much clearer ideas on the form that industrial democracy should take. One was the TUC, which was rapidly moving towards a commitment to 50 per cent worker representation at Board level; the other was the Institute for Workers' Control which, since its formation in 1968, had provided a forceful articulation of the case for self-management.

In 1973 the TUC General Council adopted an Interim Report on Industrial Democracy which, with some minor amendments, was adopted as the Movement's policy at the 1974 Conference. The report came out strongly against any general system of works' councils as these would duplicate existing trade union machinery; collective bargaining was seen as the main way to limit unilateral management prerogatives in day-to-day matters. The most important and contentious proposal, however, was the demand for 50 per cent worker representation on Supervisory Boards: joint control had become the new orthodoxy. One consequence of this revised position was that the TUC now supported the continental model of two-tier boards. For the nationalised industries this was thought likely to require only limited departures from existing practice:

> The existing nationalised boards already perform a function not dissimilar to a Supervisory Board; indeed, in certain nationalised industries there is also an executive or operating board subordinate to the main board. It is proposed that this system – which is in effect a two-tier system – is retained, but that at least the majority of the trade union representation should be made through union and TUC machinery. The proportion of the board so appointed should be one half.
>
> [*Industrial Democracy: Interim Report*
> (London: TUC, 1973) p. 39]

The best statement of the alternative view proposed by the advocates of workers' control was the one set out by the Bristol Aircraft Workers' Study Group. The TUC's interim report was attacked and the figure of 50 per cent worker-directors questioned:

> What we would ask is the significance of the 50% representation? The question surely is, does this or does it not give control? If not, it does not matter whether the representation is 5%, 10% or 50%. . . . We cannot therefore understand why the TUC documents fail even to discuss the proposition that the overall policy making body of a publicly owned industry could be com-

posed entirely of directly elected trade unionists who work in the
industry concerned and that they should be clearly answerable
and responsible to those who elected them.

[Bristol Aircraft Workers, *A New Approach to Public Ownership*
(Institute for Workers' Control pamphlet No. 43, 1973) p. 11]

The Study Group's alternative was the establishment of a Controlling Council of worker representatives elected from and by trade
unionists who work in the industry. This council would have overall control and determine policy; it would be responsible for the
appointment and dismissal of all members of an Industry Management Executive. The acceptance of Yugoslavian ideas and the
adoption of the two-tier board system produced the organisational
structure favoured by the Study Group. It was totally different
from the pattern suggested by the TUC.

Calls for experimentation dominated the literature of this period
and they were reflected in growing demands from the trade unions
themselves. Many of these took the form of extending the list of
subjects that were negotiable, but one major innovation needs
more detailed consideration: this was the introduction of worker-
directors in the British Steel Corporation that Harold Wilson referred to in the extract reproduced above. Steel was renationalised by
the 1967 Iron and Steel Act, but the worker-director scheme
resulted from a favourable interpretation of the Act and was not a
legislative requirement. The scheme grew from internal pressure
in the industry, mainly from the National Joint Craftsmen's Co-
ordinating Committee of craft unions. Twelve worker-directors
were appointed in March 1968 to the Divisional Boards from a
short-list presented by the TUC Steel Committee. On appointment
they relinquished all trade union offices. The original objectives
were three-fold: to enable a shop-floor view to be brought to the
boards; to provide a symbol of the new departure in attitudes; to
involve employees in decision-making.

The initial phase of the scheme was reviewed by the TUC Steel
Committee and BSC four years later. Two serious problems were
identified as responsible for its limited success. The first was that
worker-directors were not representative and lacked contact with
their 'constituencies'; the second was that the Divisional Boards
were away from the centre of decision-making. As a result of this
overview the scheme was changed to allow worker-directors to continue to hold union office on appointment. The selection of worker-
directors continued to be the entire responsibility of the BSC Chairman so the involvement of the rank-and-file member was negligible.

The worker-director scheme was a disappointment, but the
reasons underlying its shortcomings provide object-lessons for the

design of future schemes. A recent study has attributed the lack of success to the following factors:

> Since the nationalisation of the Steel Industry there has been an increasing tendency towards the centralisation of decision-making. In that sense the divisional boards on which the worker-directors sat were not at the centre of power. At divisional level, moreover, formal and informal meetings of full-time directors were more significant to the decision-making process than formal board meetings . . .

and

> even, however, if the board had been the locus of decision-making within BSC our analysis has suggested that there is a number of social processes related to worker representation at board level which militate against a shop floor view being heard for long in the board-room, let alone shop floor interests being actively pursued. These processes are related to selection and socialisation . . . it was clear that important members of management in their concern for academic ability, local government and broad trade union experience were seeking in worker-directors those qualities which they thought would make these new men most amenable to becoming 'normal' board members.
>
> [Brannen, Batstone, Fatchett and White, *The Worker Directors* (London: Hutchinson, 1976) p. 234]

The scheme failed to provide a channel for the expression of the views of the workforce when they conflicted with management opinion. The worker-directors were not in close touch with the shop floor; they were not necessarily involved when decisions were taken; the selection procedure made them more likely to be sympathetic to an orthodox viewpoint.

The appointment of worker-directors, if not reinforced by other changes, fits uneasily into schemes of extending industrial democracy which emphasise the 'essential bargaining' relationship outlined previously. It is not surprising, therefore, that there have been widely different attitudes amongst individual trade unions. These were fully exposed when they gave evidence to the Bullock Committee, but an early indication came with the publication of the Plowden Report on the Electricity Supply Industry in 1976. Worker representation on the Electricity Industry Boards was rejected on the grounds that it 'would have little to do with giving those working in the industry a chance to take a direct part in decisions affecting their working lives' and 'there would be no meaningful accountability to the Secretary of State and to Parliament'. Moreover:

Not all the unions in the industry supported the TUC. The strongest opposition came from two of those with greatest weight in the industry who argued that a trade union's duty to represent its members' interests, including those of members employed outside the Electricity Supply Industry, could not be reconciled with even a share in responsibility for managing the industry. It is also worth recording that little of the evidence which we received from individual employees showed a wish for representation on the Board.

[*The Structure of the Electricity Supply Industry in England and Wales*, Cmnd 6388 (London: HMSO, 1976) p. 45]

Frank Chapple, General Secretary of the Electrical, Electronic, Telecommunication and Plumbing Union, was a member of the Plowden Committee and a supporter of its conclusions.

The Plowden Committee argued that no single system of worker representation could be applied to all industries and that it should result from the expressed demands of the workers themselves. The 1974 Labour Government, in the very limited initiatives that took place before the establishment of the Bullock Committee, also took this view which became known as the 'organic' approach to the problem. The Aircraft and Shipbuilding Industries Bill required that 'each corporation shall have full regard to the need to promote industrial democracy in its undertakings and the undertakings of its subsidiaries'. No precise form of industrial democracy was prescribed. The Industry Act 1975 listed among the functions of the NEB 'promoting industrial democracy in undertakings which the Board control'. A subsequent moderation of the NEB guidelines took place in 1977 when the NEB was charged merely with making 'appropriate arrangements' to ensure that managements play their part in furthering Government policies on industrial democracy.

The most detailed statement of the Labour Government's initial viewpoint was set out in its discussion paper on worker participation in Harland and Wolff. Substantial extra funds for the shipyard, which is the biggest single employer in Northern Ireland, were announced by the Minister of State in July 1974 and he laid great emphasis on productivity improvements to be secured through worker involvement. The discussion document was circulated to all workers and, while spelling out the broad options, it emphasised that the workers should be fully involved in devising whatever scheme emerged. An unfortunate postscript demonstrates a problem central to the introduction of industrial democracy. A Board consisting of five worker-directors, five executives and five Government nominees was agreed to be the best form, but its introduction was delayed for over a year as a result of disputes between the thirteen trade unions operating at the yard over the method of electing worker-directors.

The Labour Party's 1974 election manifestos had contained an explicit commitment to legislation on industrial democracy. At the beginning of the term of office there was no clear indication of the way in which this commitment would be honoured; responsibility for worker participation seemed to involve three major Government departments – Trade, Industry and Employment – and there were clear differences of emphasis between them. The Bullock Committee was eventually established as a direct result of evidence of parliamentary frustration over lack of progress.

In January 1975, Giles Radice, a Labour backbencher, requested permission to introduce a Private Member's Bill on industrial democracy and he received the support of over 200 MPs. A procedural error on the Government Whips' part allowed the Bill to pass through a second reading unopposed and it entered the committee stage. Radice agreed to withdraw his Bill only on condition that a Committee of Inquiry was established.

In August 1975 the Trade Secretary, Peter Shore, announced that he intended to appoint the Committee 'to advise on questions relating to representation at board level in the private sector' while at the same time conducting a parallel investigation into the role of employees in relation to nationalised industries' decision-making. The parallel investigation, undertaken within the Department by a Committee under the chairmanship of Alan Lord, a civil servant, was never published as such. The main Bullock Committee, however, discussed most of the major issues relevant to the public sector – particularly if industrial democracy is viewed as a problem concerned with the relationship between managers and managed rather than labour and capital.

The Committee's membership was announced in December 1975. Lord Bullock, Master of St Catherine's College, Oxford, was named as Chairman; Jack Jones, General Secretary of the Transport and General Workers Union, and David Lea, Secretary of the TUC Economic Department, were two members who were closely associated with the new TUC orthodoxy. The terms of reference, which received a great deal of criticism, amounted to an endorsement of the TUC position:

> Accepting the need for a radical extension of industrial democracy in the control of companies by means of representation on boards of directors, and accepting the essential role of trade union organisations in this process, to consider how such an extension can best be achieved, taking into account in particular the proposals of the Trades Union Congress report on industrial democracy as well as experience in Britain, the EEC and other countries. Having regard to the interests of the national economy,

employees, investors, and consumers to analyse the implications of such representation for the efficient management of companies and for company law.

With these terms of reference it was scarcely surprising that the majority of the Committee supported the principle of worker representation on boards. Neither was it surprising, since the Committee balanced three trade unionists with three industrialists, that a minority report was produced.

The majority report recommended that boards should be reconstituted to include an equal number of employee and shareholder representatives with a smaller third group who would be acceptable to the other two. Two-tier boards were dismissed in favour of unitary boards and the majority argued that all directors should have the same responsibilities. All employees in a company would vote on whether the system should be introduced but only recognised unions could begin the process. The majority recommended that arrangements for the selection of worker-directors would then be made by a joint union committee, the Joint Representation Committee. Finally, the report recommended the establishment of an Industrial Democracy Commission to overview the whole process. The minority report dissented on the following grounds: that the remit was unsatisfactory; that satisfactory systems of participation required prior development below board level; that worker representation should take the form of minority representation on a Supervisory Board in a two-tier system and that worker-directors should be chosen by all the employees.

The Bullock Report contained a comprehensive analysis of the problems of putting worker representatives on company boards. Minority representation was rejected as 'it leaves control of major decisions and of the decision-making process in the hands of the shareholder representatives and management and therefore does not fundamentally change the way in which decisions are reached or the premises on which they are based' [*Report of the Committee of Inquiry on Industrial Democracy*, Cmnd 6706 (London: HMSO, 1977) p. 94], but co-opted directors were preferred to a fifty–fifty board as they would bring outside expertise to the company and reduce polarisation between the blocks of worker and shareholder directors.

The central role of the trade unions in any realistic progress to industrial democracy was defended:

Since trade unions are necessary to ensure that employees have an effective voice in decision-making both within the company and within the wider society, we wish to ensure that board level representation is designed in such a way that it does not undermine the unions' representative capacity . . .

and trade union machinery

> would provide the expertise and independent strength necessary
> to support employee representatives and to enable them to play
> an effective role in decision-making on the board. It would also
> provide an established and trusted channel of communication to
> and from the shop floor through which employee representatives
> could keep in touch with their constituents.
>
> [Ibid., p. 111]

Unitary boards were preferred to two-tier boards since:

> It is a mistake to suppose that there is some easy distinction to
> be drawn between the functions of a board of directors and those
> of senior executives. We fear that attempts to define such a dis-
> tinction in United Kingdom law could have one of two main
> consequences: either it would, in its desire to preserve the free-
> dom of management, so delimit the powers of the board on which
> employees are represented that employee participation in decision-
> making would be very restricted; or it would impose strains and
> tensions on decision-making at top level, by requiring the adop-
> tion of an alien and rigid board structure. . . .
>
> [Ibid., p. 77]

The case for directors appointed to represent the consumer interest
was dismissed:

> Consumer interests must continue to be protected, as they are
> now, against the action of industrial enterprises, but the way to
> do this is through legislation and through the existing consumer
> organisations, rather than by involving consumers in the running
> of companies. The involvement of employees and shareholders
> in a company is different in kind from that of consumers. Further-
> more, we see serious practical difficulties in achieving satisfactory
> representation of consumers on boards. Generally speaking there
> is no recognisable consumer constituency equivalent to that of
> employees and shareholders and therefore no way in which a
> guardian of consumer interests could be appointed to the board
> through representative machinery.
>
> [Ibid., p. 55]

The report also discussed, somewhat briefly, possible problems arising from the conflicts of worker representation with collective bargaining and difficulties resulting from management attitudes.

The Bullock Committee did not, however, contain a comprehensive review of the alternative ways of promoting industrial democracy. Its terms of reference were too restrictive to permit it to do so. Although the Committee proclaimed that the terms 'have not however precluded us from considering the wider aspects of participation in decision-making', the emphasis on board level changes worked to the detriment of broader examination that could have provoked a wider-ranging debate. The Committee did not discuss industrial democracy 'in terms of enterprises managed solely for the benefit of employees' – thus sidestepping the issue of workers' control. Equally importantly, the Committee dismissed the evidence that it received about job enrichment and work restructuring as peripheral to the discussion.

A well-orchestrated public row followed the publication of Bullock. What is of importance is that the opposition to the majority recommendations came not only from supporters of traditional management authority, but also from within the trade union movement. The TUC position was far less certain than a simple reading of their 1973 report would suggest. At the 1974 Congress wide support was secured for a composite motion, moved by the Amalgamated Union of Engineering Workers, which read:

> Congress reaffirms that the over-riding role of the unions is the advancement of the interests of their members. It therefore requires that any extension of trade union participation in industrial management shall be, and seen to be, an extension of collective bargaining and shall in no sense compromise the union's role as here defined. Recognising that the best way to strengthen industrial democracy is to strengthen and extend the area of collective bargaining giving union representatives increased control over elements of management including dismissals, discipline, introduction of new techniques, forward planning of manpower rationalisation etc., Congress rejects the mandatory imposition of Supervisory Boards with worker-directors and calls for a more flexible approach giving statutory backing to the right to negotiate on these major issues, but relating the control more directly to collective bargaining machinery.

This resolution was scarcely compatible with the support for the new TUC position of parity worker representation on boards that was endorsed at the same Congress.

The 'more flexible approach' offered by Bullock was of the take-it-or-leave-it variety: trade unions could take advantage of or ignore the opportunity of selecting worker-directors. This was unacceptable to the Electrical, Electronic, Telecommunication and Plumbing Union, which had already rejected worker-directors in the Electricity Industry. Its Executive Council was scathing in its condemnation of Bullock, arguing:

> The conclusions of the Bullock Committee are not in line with this union, nor indeed with that of the TUC as expressed at Congress. The terms of reference and the composition of the Committee made it inevitable that this predetermined result would occur. It will not solve the deep and underlying problems of Britain, nor will it advance the cause of genuine industrial democracy. We do not align ourselves with those whose objections are based on opposition to any advances of workers' influence in decision-making, nor those whose main concern appears to be the possible redundancy of 6000 directors. The real extension of democracy in industry will come through the natural extension of collective bargaining and not through the elevation of a few individuals to boards of management.

The EETPU had argued in its evidence to Bullock that 50 per cent trade union representation on boards would convey the impression that the management had captured or absorbed the trade unions; in their view it was vital that the traditional role of independent trade union power as a countervailing force was maintained and strengthened.

Other criticism of the Bullock conclusions from within the trade union movement were less forthright. The General and Municipal Workers' Union, for example, in its evidence had favoured:

> A mandatory general obligation on company management and directors to consult and negotiate with trade unions on all major decisions involving investment, closures, mergers, organisation changes and redeployment. But we believe the precise machinery should be left to negotiation between the employer and the recognised trade unions within the companies.

The union, like the EETPU, rejected the imposition of any specific form of mechanism. Much greater disclosure of information to union negotiators was a prerequisite for a successful extension of industrial democracy along the lines proposed by the union, but Bullock did not recommend any changes in the relevant law.

The Bullock Committee reported in January 1977, although its conclusions were widely publicised several weeks earlier. The Secretary of State for Trade announced the Government's intention to bring forward legislative proposals after consultation; at the same time he stated that employees in nationalised industries would also be given the right to representation at board level. Since then the debate has continued and at the same time some of the nationalised industries have introduced their own arrangements. The Post Office Corporation has introduced a Bullock-style board with seven management directors, seven union directors and five outside directors; the British Steel Corporation is considering the introduction of a Steel Council which would be constituted in a similar way; British Aerospace, given a statutory duty to report on progress towards industrial democracy within three months of vesting day, has recommended a four-tier structure of joint consultative councils.

The different methods and rates of progress introduced in the different industries should not be condemned out of hand. Once it is accepted that the relationship between management and unions is essentially a bargaining relationship, the form of industrial democracy itself should be resolved by negotiation. If this is what is meant by an 'organic' arrangement, it should be supported. The main role for the Government is then to create a climate, and a legislative background, which encourages effective change through bargaining.

It was unfortunate that the restrictive remit of the Bullock Committee precluded a wider examination of these issues; it will be tragic if the ensuing debate centres exclusively round worker representation on the boards of public and private companies. Experience in the British Steel Corporation has shown that the appointment of worker-directors alone will not lead to a shift in power – but this is scarcely surprising. Worker representation on the boards must, at the very least, be part of an overall strategy. On the other hand, the importance of worker-directors as a guarantee of access to information should not be understated.

What the Labour Movement has so far failed to undertake is a full appraisal of the relative merits of alternative ways of obtaining a dispersion of power. The methods of promoting industrial democracy have, all too often, been seen as objectives in themselves. Means have been confused with ends and the debate has suffered as a consequence.

4 Acting and Reacting: Three Case Studies

'It's not fair', interrupted John. 'I promised Rodney Merrivale fifteen conkers if he'd do my algebra for me.' 'And did he do it?' asked father, suddenly serious. 'Yes,' complained John, 'but if I give him fifteen conkers I'll have such a measly few left for myself.' 'That's easy,' said father brightening. 'Tell him that the John Bedworth for whom he did the algebra has gone into liquidation; that you have taken over the conker division trading as John Bedworth (1971) Ltd., and that he'll have to renegotiate the contract.' 'Gosh,' gasped John, 'Can one do that? Would Mr. Heath approve?' 'Of course, silly,' smiled father 'we do it all the time. It's called being realistic.'

[From J. D. Crispin's winning entry to a 1971 *New Statesman* competition]

The case studies set out in this chapter are intended to illustrate some of the problems inherent in developing a policy for common ownership in the 1970s. The collapse of Rolls-Royce occurred when a Conservative Government was in power; the problems of change in the Steel Industry have remained throughout Labour and Conservative administrations; the resurgence in interest in worker co-operatives has taken place under a Labour Government. Taken together, they illustrate the fragility of any industrial policy based on an over-dogmatic approach. They also demonstrate that events have a way of running ahead of policy formulation.

The case studies also raise questions on the potential role that common ownership can fulfil. The first two case studies prompt the question of how much difference nationalisation has made in practical terms in the industries concerned. One major problem that occurs in industrial policy is highlighted: the way that change can have a severe impact on particular sectors and particular communities. Expansion in one area of industrial activity can sometimes only take place at the expense of contraction in another. This, and other harsh facts of industrial life, is true regardless of the pattern of ownership.

THE COLLAPSE OF ROLLS-ROYCE

During a general election public ownership becomes a major political issue irrespective of the actual industrial changes likely to be enacted by the elected Government. In 1970 the Labour Party promised to remove the restriction on the activities of existing nationalised industries, to establish joint public–private sector ventures and to create a Holding and Development Company. The Conservative manifesto was abrasive in tone, stating that an incoming Conservative Government would be totally opposed to any further nationalisation. This strident position was echoed throughout the campaign – although few actual measures designed to alter the boundaries of the public sector were mentioned.

The Conservatives' ideological commitment to the industrial survival of the fittest was maintained in office. John Davies, Secretary for Trade and Industry, referred, in November 1970, to the need of the country to gear its policies to the great majority of the people, who are not lame ducks. Subsequent events proved that his position was untenable. Only one practical expression of this aggressive competition policy was implemented: some profitable subsidiaries of the public corporations were 'hived-off'. Legislation was passed in July 1971 for the denationalisation and disposal of over 200 licensed premises in Carlisle and Scotland; they had been taken in public ownership almost accidentally as a way of controlling alcohol consumption in the munitions factories in the First World War. Certain assets held by the Transport Holding Company, notably the travel agency business of Thomas Cook & Son, were put up for sale in the same year. The British Steel Corporation disposed of some brick-making, tool and tool-steel works, and high carbon and mild steel wire interests; the National Coal Board sold its brickworks. All the changes, however, were peripheral, and seen at the time to be so, compared with the traumatic reversal of Conservative policy caused by the collapse of Rolls-Royce in February 1971.

At the time of the collapse Rolls-Royce employed 80,000 people and was Britain's fourteenth largest company in employment terms. Its importance transcended its size. It had for so long represented what was best in British engineering and too much prestige was at stake for it to be allowed to collapse. For years the name of Rolls-Royce had been associated with excellence and the company had a history of continued growth through technical superiority.

In 1904 Henry Royce and Charles Rolls agreed to manufacture and sell a new car. Two years later the company was formed and the Silver Ghost appeared; it established the company as the symbol of luxury motoring and it has remained so ever since. During the first world war Rolls-Royce diversified into armoured cars and aero-engines. T. E. Lawrence (Lawrence of Arabia) requisitioned nine of the cars and commented that 'A Rolls in the desert was above rubies.' It was the move into aero-engines that was to have such a devastating impact on the company in the future. The post-war surge in the demand for air-flight ensured that this side of the company's activities expanded: when the first regular London-Paris flights were introduced they were powered with Rolls-Royce engines and so was Alcock and Brown's pioneer transatlantic crossing. The company's biggest achievement came with the development of the Merlin engine which powered almost all the British planes in the Second World War, including the Hurricanes and Spitfires.

The Rolls-Royce jet engine was developed in the early 1940s. By the middle of the 1960s this part of the company's activities was to dwarf all the others as Rolls-Royce emerged to become the market leader. At the time of the collapse the other divisions, which included motor-cars, diesel engines, industrial and marine gas turbines, oil engines and small engines, accounted together for less than a fifth of the combined activities. [For a detailed account of the company history see Robert Gray, *Rolls on the Rocks* (London: Compton Press, 1971)]

The company's eventual difficulties were caused by their contractual obligation to supply the RB211 engine to the Lockheed Corporation of America. The market for aeroplanes was dominated by the American suppliers, whose defence contracts guaranteed long production runs. Competition for aero-engines was particularly fierce, and in securing the Lockheed contract Rolls-Royce had to undercut the major American suppliers, who were aided by a protective import duty.

In March 1968 a tripartite deal involving Rolls-Royce, Lockheed and three airlines was announced; a deal which was supported by the Labour Government then in power. The RB211 represented a breakthrough in quieter thrust technology, the blades were made of a new carbon fibre material and it was altogether technically superior to the product of American competitors. The contract signed was a long and detailed document but subsequent events showed that the penalty clauses were too severe and that there was insufficient provision for inflation.

It was apparent over the next two years that a series of production problems were causing delays and that the contract would need renegotiation. In November 1970 just one week after John Davies' 'lame duck' statement the Government announced additional launching aid up to a maximum of £42 million to help Rolls-Royce meet the inflated cost of the engine. The clearing banks announced a loan of a further £18 million. These sums were subject to 'a further check of the figures by independent accountants, to satisfactory contractual arrangements, and to limitation for a period of any distribution on the company's ordinary share capital'.

Three months later an internal reappraisal forced Rolls-Royce management to conclude that even the additional £42 million was insufficient to permit the company to continue trading and meet its commitments. On the morning of 5 February 1971 trading in Rolls-Royce shares was suspended and a receiver appointed for the company and its four subsidiaries. Two days earlier rumours of the collapse had led to £5 million being wiped off the value of the company shares; on the day of the collapse, the FT share index, which did not even include Rolls-Royce, fell nine points.

The repercussions of the company's failure were felt most strongly amongst its suppliers. Rolls-Royce debts to other companies were estimated to exceed £200 million. Joseph Lucas Ltd were owed about £7 million and predicted a minimum of 3000 redundancies as a result of the Rolls-Royce failure. The impact was expected to be especially severe in Derby where local debts were estimated at over £6·8 million. Particularly poignant were the problems faced by the company's window cleaners who were owed £16,000 and for the last twenty-five years had had no contract other than Rolls-Royce. Like all major companies Rolls-Royce operations were concentrated in a few areas where the local economy was heavily dependent on their success. The Bishop of Derby was prompted to write to *The Times* to argue that:

> It is reliably estimated that in Derby itself one out of every three people has a direct connection with Rolls-Royce. 60% of those employed by the firm in Derby are working on the RB211. If this is not continued the consequences locally in personal and family distress will be appalling and it is not only Derby which will suffer through prolonged unemployment on a vast scale. Many other areas of the country will be affected as well and the knowledge, skills and experience of numerous individuals will be wasted.
>
> [*The Times*, 17 February 1971]

The Conservative Cabinet's immediate reaction to the crash was to allow the company to go bankrupt, with the intention of nationalising the aero-engine interests and cancelling the financial liabilities resulting from the RB211 contract. Lockheed could no longer insist on the company honouring its penalty clauses and this provoked an angry reaction from several sources. Lockheed's Chairman referred to his Board's complete surprise at the precipitate decision made by the Rolls-Royce Board and the withdrawal of the British Government's financial support. Opposition spokesmen expressed their surprise at the Government's decision to allow the company's collapse less than 100 days after underwriting it with a further £60 million loan.

The biggest problem faced by the Government was the necessity of convincing its backbench supporters that nationalisation was necessary. The Minister of Aviation Supply announced in Parliament on the day after the collapse that:

> To ensure continuity of those activities of Rolls-Royce which are important to our national defence, to our collaborative programmes with other countries and to many airforces and civil airlines all over the world, the Government has decided to acquire such assets of the aero-engine and marine and industrial gas turbine engine divisions of the company as may be essential for these purposes.
>
> [*Hansard*, 4 February 1971, col 1922]

The Minister could offer limited comfort to his backbenchers. The Government excluded the motor-car and oil engine division from the nationalisation package and, as was revealed in answer to a backbench question, it was the Government's stated intention to put the company on a viable footing and return it to private enterprise as soon as possible.

The Rolls-Royce (Purchase) Bill was due for its second reading a week later and a revolt from right-wing Conservatives was expected. In the event the revolt was easily extinguished: an amendment to the Bill designed to place a time limit on Government ownership was withdrawn following an assurance that it was the Government's desire to bring in the maximum private participation as soon as possible. Conservative backbenchers were also influenced by the argument that the Bill could not be altered as it was tightly drawn to frustrate opposition amendments for nationalisation of the entire company assets.

The real problem facing the dogmatic opponents of public ownership was the absence of alternative solutions. The Government had decided that it was cheaper to let the company collapse and purchase the assets than to continue to sustain it until the RB211 contract was complete; to the outside observer this appeared to be a cynical attempt to put the taxpayer's interests above those of the creditors. Everyone agreed that something needed to be done. The defence and international commitments of the company were stressed by the Government; the impact on employment was emphasised by the trade unions; the disproportionate effect on some communities was voiced by the local authorities. The form of rescue most acceptable to the Conservative ideologists was ruled out:

> It may be argued by some of those who are opposed to what the Government have done that it would have been possible to allow and encourage other private companies or another private company to take over Rolls-Royce. In the view of the Government it would not have been possible in the time available, even if there

had been a company with such resources at its command. There would not have been time to make arrangements which would have both kept confidence and ensured the continuation of these important defence projects. The delay to these projects might well have been fatal.

[Lord Carrington, Secretary of State for Defence, *Hansard* (House of Lords), 15 February 1971, cols 360–1]

The subsequent history of Rolls-Royce is well documented. A new company, Rolls-Royce (1971) Ltd, was created to take over the business acquired by the Government. Negotiations took place with Lockheed on the RB211 in the following month; Lockheed agreed to a new price for the engine and the Government financed the development work needed to complete the project. The car division of the company was sold as the Rolls-Royce Motor Group and, in the context of the British motor industry, has since proved highly successful. Eventually, five years after the collapse, Rolls-Royce (1971) Ltd was allowed to drop the date from its title and trade as Rolls-Royce Ltd.

The failure of the company was attributed at the time to commercial misjudgement, and there was no shortage of good advice available after the event:

Never enter into fixed price contracts in an inflationary period. Never set a fixed price on an unforeseeable technological development. Never sign a contract with a penalty clause disproportionate to your expected profit. Never put yourself into a position where one contract can ruin your business. These were the rules Rolls-Royce disobeyed.

[*The Times* leader, 5 February 1971]

It also became accepted wisdom that the company was too decentralised and was heavily overweighted with engineering skills – 80 per cent of the managers on the aero-engine side were engineers – to the detriment of commercial expertise. Since the failure was on a technological gamble this preponderance of engineers should not have proved a handicap. All the retrospective diagnoses were so much humbug. The fact is that Rolls-Royce were selling in a cutthroat market and needed to achieve and maintain a frightening rate of technical progress to compete with their American counterparts. The contract itself may have been a misjudgement, but the development of the RB211 was not a function of the company's commercial expertise.

The lessons to be drawn from Rolls-Royce are not comforting. Once a decision has been made by a Government to remain in high technology it must face the consequences whether the industry is

publicly or privately owned. There is not the slightest evidence
that the story of Rolls-Royce would have been significantly different
if the company had been nationalised in 1945 – except that the
Government would have shown more scruples in renegotiating the
contract. The escalating costs of the RB211 programme would have
resulted in a public scandal but the combination of the defence and
international commitments, and the disastrous impact of closure on
the communities where its factories were located, would have
obliged the Government to save the company from extinction.
Before nationalisation an unnamed senior executive of Rolls-Royce
was quoted as describing the job of the financial director as 'telling
us when we go to the Government for more money'.

The American economist, J. K. Galbraith, has argued that major
defence contractors are for all practical purposes part of the public
sector. He regards them as a vital part of the 'planning' as opposed
to 'market' system. On the question of company collapses in the
private sector he had this to say:

> Above a certain size, it is now evident, no industrial corporation
> can be allowed to go out of business. It still happens in Samuel-
> son but not in real life. The effect on workers, customers, mana-
> gers and creditors is too great. Nothing more wonderfully reveals
> the flexibility of the human mind than the speed with which the
> most devout free enterpriser–industrialist or banker – converts
> to socialism when this is the only chance for the survival of the
> firm or the recovery of loans.
>
> ['The Economic Problems of the Left', *New Statesman*,
> 20 February 1976, p. 218]

CHANGE IN THE STEEL INDUSTRY

Of all the basic industries nationalised since the war, steel has
caused the most political controversy. Together with parts of the
road-haulage industry it was denationalised by the Conservatives in
1951 and its renationalisation under the following Labour Government was the occasion of a well-orchestrated national publicity
campaign by the opponents of public ownership. Politically the
ownership of the industry has always been a most sensitive issue
because, although it is unquestionably a 'commanding height' of
the economy, the arguments against private enterprise are more
subtle than those that apply to other industries. The nationalisation
of electricity and gas followed the publication of Governmental
reports critical of their performance – the Weir Committee (1926)
and the McGowan Committee (1936) in electricity and the Hey-
worth Committee (1944) in the case of gas. The shortcomings of

the steel industry's operation under private ownership were less easily demonstrable, but they formed the basis of the case for nationalisation.

The private steelowners claimed that the industry was highly competitive. The advocates of nationalisation argued that agreements between the companies made the industry an effective monopoly and, moreover, an inefficient one. Competition was a charade and, since the potential advantages of unified ownership were denied, the customer was getting the worst of both worlds. The extent to which public ownership has aided the reorganisation of the industry is the subject of this case study.

The argument that efficiency in the steel industry is related to the economics of scale, the reduction in unit costs possible under large-scale production, has always been accepted. In 1945 the industry was fragmented: over fifty companies included the production of steel among their interests, but the majority of these were small-scale producers. The largest company in the industry, the United Steel Companies Ltd, controlled only 13 per cent of the national output. The industry recognised the problems caused by this dispersed pattern of ownership and in a report which was subsequently published by the Government specifically stated that the desired future pattern of the industry was to be gained by the closing of small, obsolete works, the rationalisation of finished steels, and the construction of three major new integrated works. [*Reports by the British Iron and Steel Federation and the Joint Iron Council to the Ministry of Supply,* Cmd 6811 (1946)]

The major developments outlined were to take place at Clydeside, Northamptonshire and Port Talbot. In the event only the Port Talbot development was undertaken and this led to the creation of a new Steel Company of Wales in 1947. The Scottish industry ignored the Clydeside proposals; both the companies who were likely to be involved in the Northamptonshire project were already committed to improving operations elsewhere. The steel industry had sidestepped its first post-war opportunity for modernisation.

The second opportunity came, ironically, as a result of denationalisation. In February 1951 the industry was nationalised; in October 1951 the new Conservative Government began the process of denationalisation: a Holdings and Realisation Agency was established to supervise the return to private ownership as soon as possible. If the Agency had been encouraged to rationalise the industry it could have retained the less economic works for eventual closure and taken the modernisation plans of the eventual purchaser into consideration as a criterion for the disposal of the assets. In fact the attractive lots were sold first and the industry reappeared in much the same form. No purchaser was found for Richard Thomas & Baldwin in South Wales and it remained in public ownership throughout the fifties and early sixties.

The performance of the industry in the 1950s and early 1960s became one of the major issues in the 1964 and 1966 general election campaigns. Supporters of nationalisation claimed that the industry had failed to reorganise; opponents argued that the limited amount of Government intervention that had taken place was positively detrimental to the public interest – it had been carried out against a background of the companies competing for aid. The Labour Party's case for nationalisation was made most succinctly in a small guide for speakers which was issued six months before the general election and expanded in a Fabian Society pamphlet published a year later:

> In its post-war development plan published in 1946 the Iron and Steel Federation suggested that a considerable amount of existing steel capacity should be scrapped. But not only were the industry's proposals less radical than its analysis, much of its plan was never carried out. Consequently, plants which should have been scrapped were often renovated and enlarged – not because the companies were seriously worried about redundancies – a legitimate concern – but because of the industry's inertia, its ownership structure and the inadequacy of its expansion plans.
>
> [*Ammunition: Steel* (The Labour Party: 1964) p. 20]

> Under public ownership it will be possible to concentrate new investment on a small number of plants. At present, because firms are in 'competition' with each other, and because they all try to maintain or increase their share of the market, expansion takes place across the board. Hence every firm is able to grow a little but no firm is able to grow a lot. As a result nobody obtains the economies of scale which would be possible if expansion was concentrated on certain plants. This has become particularly important now that the demand for steel is no longer growing as fast as it was.
>
> [Richard Pryke, *Why Steel* (London: Fabian Research Series No. 248, 1965) pp. 29–30]

This argument received support from an unexpected quarter. In 1966 the British Iron and Steel Federation set up a Development Co-ordinating Committee and its Stage I report, subsequently known as the Benson Report, put the case for the rationalisation of capacity. The Committee concluded that production should be concentrated at a number of larger sites and that their development would be hampered unless some existing capacity was withdrawn. The Stage II Report would have analysed the implications of the strategy for the companies; in the event it was never published.

The Benson Committee was formed as a defensive reaction against nationalisation and argued that the rationalisation proposals would be better carried out under private ownership. Some mergers did take place but they were trivial in the context of the industry as a whole.

The industry was renationalised in 1967. The Iron and Steel Act transferred the fourteen largest crude steel companies to public ownership and created, in terms of output, the second largest steel company in the non-communist world. An organising committee for the new British Steel Corporation had been established in the previous year and reported that initially the new industry would be organised in four regional groupings. This structure was unlikely to aid reorganisation: pre-emptive strikes at the available investment capital were made within the first eighteen months when the Scottish and Midlands Group independently announced their expansion plans. Tighter control at the centre was needed and this came in 1969 when the Steel Corporation published two reports on reorganisation. As a result of these reports four new steel divisions and an engineering and a chemical division were created. Functional organisation replaced geographical organisation.

With this more centralised structure it was possible for BSC to introduce corporate planning procedures to determine the best long-term strategy for the industry – ignoring regional or company pleading for special expansion projects. A first corporate plan, involving a massive increase in crude steel capacity, was presented to the Government in February 1971. It was rejected by the Minister and a Joint Study Group made up of BSC management and civil servants was established in 1971 – a first indication that the relationship between the Government and the industry was deteriorating. Following the Joint Study Group's deliberations and a report from McKinsey, a firm of management consultants retained by the Study Group, BSC were invited to produce a new long-term strategy.

The resulting strategy favoured by BSC involved expansion at five existing sites and the establishment of a new steel complex at Teesside. The Conservative Government, faced with the need to determine a policy for rationalisation, prevaricated for two years. Eventually the plan was endorsed in a White Paper which was published in February 1973. After the years of indecision this was an instant decision: Peter Walker apparently made up his mind on the plan and persuaded the Cabinet to agree to BSC's proposals within three weeks of his arrival at the Department of Trade and Industry. The most contentious aspect of the proposals concerned the redundancies and the White Paper had this to say:

Modernisation means fewer jobs, but is essential if the remaining jobs are to be securely based. Labour productivity in the new

Teesside works is expected to be about 800 tonnes a year, as against 250 tonnes in BSC's best present works. BSC estimates that full implementation of the new developments and closures in the strategy should more than double average labour productivity and reduce manpower by about 50,000. Closures already announced before the strategy was settled account for over 20,000 of this reduction. The decision on the strategy means an additional 30,000 net job losses, mainly in the second half of the decade. The effect will be severe in certain places, but the annual impact overall will not be out of proportion with the average rate of reduction in employment since nationalisation; it will be markedly below the 23,000 fall in the Corporation's manpower in the single year ending 31 March 1972.

> [White Paper, *British Steel Corporation: Ten Year Development Strategy,* Cmnd 5226 (London: HMSO, 1973) pp. 12–13]

The first half of the last sentence of the above quotation was the most important. The overall loss in jobs would not be out of proportion with the changes that had occurred in other public sector industries, but the effect on some communities would be devastating. The opposition to the strategy was to come from those works and the steel workers had the support of the local authorities and the community at large.

The trade unions in the steel industry reacted by holding a one-day conference in 1973 to discuss the White Paper and passed a resolution which, whilst recognising the need to develop a modern and competitive steel industry in the interests of the industry's prosperity and that of its workpeople and in the interests of the national economy, went on to demand that:

Before any final decision on plant closures is taken, each prospective closure shall be investigated in depth by a Committee composed of representatives of the British Steel Corporation and of the trade unions of which the employees concerned are members. These investigations should include close consideration of the economic and social consequences arising and no plant shall be closed until a searching examination of all possible means of preventing or delaying the closure has revealed that there is no alternative. Should these investigations conclude that a plant closure is inevitable such closure shall not take place until satisfactory job opportunities have been made available in the locality for all those who will be made redundant, and in this connection special attention is drawn to the major responsibility which the Government bears.

The strategy of investigating each closure in depth was the one chosen by the Labour Government when it was returned to power in February 1974. Faced with the politically explosive problem of plant closures, and the possibility of nationalist groups in Wales and Scotland making considerable political capital, Tony Benn at the Department of Industry announced that a special review committee would be established under Lord Beswick, Minister of State for Industry. The review would take the form of discussions with the TUC and BSC and Lord Beswick was given the Herculean task of discovering 'how best to plan for an efficient and expanding Steel Industry, essential for the country as a whole and which alone can provide long-term assurance of employment to steelworkers, while reducing to a minimum the disturbance to the life and livelihood of steelworkers and their communities'. In its Annual Report for 1973/4 BSC tartly commented that it 'continues to believe that these rationalisation proposals are essential for the future prosperity of its operators and thus for the best long-term security of employment for its retained and future workforce'. This was less than fair. Although the Corporation was committed to the strategy, falling demand and rising costs had raised questions, inside and outside the industry, about its viability.

The Beswick review reported in two stages. In February 1975 the conclusions on the steel industry in England and Wales were announced: about 13,500 jobs were reprieved by deferring plant closures and by creating new opportunities in locations where the BSC planned rundowns were accepted. The Scottish review was completed six months later and the net job loss in Scotland consequent on BSC plans was reduced from 6500 to 2100.

The Beswick review was a compromise which left no one completely happy. The steel industry management, unions and consumers had all, from their different viewpoints, grounds for complaint. The dilemmas faced by the Government were real, however, and it is all too easy to underestimate the pressures that they were facing at the time. A consideration of the implications that the BSC strategy would have on the steel industry in Wales provides a good illustration of the uninviting options open.

Two plants in Wales, Port Talbot and Llanwern, would have benefited considerably from the BSC Corporate Plan. On the other hand the loss in jobs would have been severe at three other sites: East Moors (Cardiff), Shotton and Ebbw Vale. The Beswick review offered some comfort. The closure of East Moors was deferred until January 1980; this saved the Government from acute political embarrassment since the Cardiff steelworkers had threatened to attempt to run the works as a co-operative in the event of closure. On the other hand the Beswick Committee endorsed the closure of Ebbw Vale, which led to Michael Foot, the Secretary of State for Employment and the local Member of Parliament, facing an angry and hostile reception from his constituents.

The Beswick decision on Shotton was delayed. BSC were invited to defer their proposed closure to 1980/81 while a further study was undertaken. The result of the study was expected in August, at the time of the second report, but was deferred again. No firm decision had been taken by April 1976 when Sir Monty Finniston, Chairman of BSC, argued, in the course of giving evidence to the Select Committee on Nationalised Industries, that it was essential that approval should be given for the transfer of steel making from Shotton to Port Talbot. The extent to which the expansion of Port Talbot and the retention of Shotton are alternatives has always been a matter of dispute between the Steel Corporation and the Government. In July of the same year the Secretary of State announced that the Steel Corporation could proceed with the Port Talbot scheme, but that the Corporation had been asked to carry out yet another review at Shotton. Finally in March 1977 the Government announced that the Corporation had withdrawn their closure proposals for Shotton since 'the Corporation believe that to close Shotton's iron and steel making capacity when prospects are uncertain and while Port Talbot is being built up over an extended period might risk a shortage'.

A decision to close Shotton would have been highly contentious. The plant is sited on the Dee estuary in North Wales and the whole community was directly threatened by the closure proposal. The County Council had estimated the total job loss at 9000: 6450 in the works itself, 1800 in the docks and a local colliery, and a further 1000 in other dependent contracting firms. Courtaulds had recently decided to make 1500 people redundant at a nearby textile works and the Shotton closure would have driven male unemployment on Deeside to over 25 per cent.

Effectively the closure proposals inherent in the BSC Corporate Plans were taken out of the Corporation's hands and the Government made the best political compromise that it could. Relationships between the Government and the Corporation deteriorated even further while the Beswick review was in progress. They reached a nadir when, during the course of a dinner with industrial correspondents held shortly after the first Beswick report, Sir Monty Finniston disclosed that to ensure the profitability of the Corporation the labour force should be cut by 10 per cent or 22,000 men. The result was the most open and public row ever involving the Chairman of a nationalised industry and the Government. Public letters were exchanged between Sir Monty and Tony Benn, the Secretary of State, in an attempt to clarify their roles culminating in the latter openly asking the BSC Chairman 'for an absolutely clear assurance that you will take no action to meet the recession that would in any way pre-empt the outcome of the Government's closure review or inhibit BSC's ability to meet demand once the situation improves'. Sir Monty Finniston was replaced as BSC Chairman in the following year.

The way that the ragged interface between Government and the nationalised industry can lead to an uneasy relationship is apparent from the BSC experience – although the subsequent period witnessed a dramatic improvement in relationships, in part due to changes in the BSC Board. The main lesson to be drawn, however, concerns the limitations on public ownership as a vehicle for change. Pious hopes were expressed in the pre-nationalisation days on the ease in which the transformation could be made: 'The risk of redundancy can be reduced because steel nationalisation will make it easier to plan the industry. For instance, when the industry is nationalised the elimination of old capacity will be planned and so phased over a considerable period' [*Ammunition: Steel*, op. cit., p. 45]; 'Under nationalisation, however, the risk of redundancy can be reduced because the labour requirements of the industry can be properly planned. Instead of men being laid off, the labour force can, where necessary, be run down through natural wastage'. [*Why Steel*, op. cit., p. 33] Nationalisation is capable of easing the problem of redundancy; it is also capable of achieving economies of scale through unified ownership. It cannot necessarily achieve both at the same time.

One other disturbing aspect of the BSC experience also needs to be considered. It is too easy to seek to apportion blame by identifying scapegoats. In the steel industry convenient scapegoats have been the trade unions (blamed by the right-wing newspapers), the management (blamed by some Members of Parliament), and the Government (blamed by virtually everyone). Unquestionably there have been occasions when change could have been handled better, and BSC management has been maladroit, but the reaction of the other groups was understandable given their standpoint. It was the underlying problem itself that caused the difficulties.

THE MOTOR-CYCLE CO-OPERATIVE

Although the motor-cycle co-operative at Meriden, in Warwickshire, was a product of the economic forces of the 1970s, co-operation in industry has always been an important historic strand in British socialism. Its origins are linked with the reforming work undertaken by the philanthropist Robert Owen in the first half of the nineteenth century. The characteristic pattern of consumer co-operation in Britain was established by the Rochdale Pioneers, whose society was started in 1844. As well as expanding the activities of their own society, the Pioneers assisted with the development of other societies and initiated efforts to start wholesale trading activities. The retail side of the movement has prospered and the producer co-operatives have not. Only about twenty producer co-operatives have survived and the most successful of these is Equity Shoes of Leicester, which employs some 200 people.

To be considered a co-operative an organisation must, strictly speaking, be registered under the Industrial and Provident Societies Act. The new worker co-operatives of the 1970s have, however, all been registered under the Companies Act. The Industrial and Provident Societies Act, which first entered the statute book in 1852, is the legal expression of the principles practised at Rochdale. At the heart is an explicit rejection of undertaking a business 'with the object of making profits mainly for the payment of interest, dividends or bonuses òn money invested or deposited with or lent to the society or any other purpose'. Although the new co-operatives are not registered under the Act they satisfy many of the Rochdale principles. Their organisation is determined by the workers instead of the workers being expected to conform with the organisation. On the Yugoslavian pattern it is the workers themselves who are the ultimate controlling body.

The new worker co-operatives have understandably an enormous appeal for the Labour idealist, but it would be wrong to over-romanticise about their origins: the political sympathies of their leadership were an essential ingredient, but the determined refusal of their workforce to accept the arbitrary loss of their livelihood was the most powerful force leading to their creation. The strength of the reaction to redundancy from the shop floor has transformed industrial politics in the 1970s. One commentator has identified 102 separate factory occupations that occurred over a three-year period between 1971 and 1974 – a high proportion of these were in defence of employment. [A. J. Mills, 'Factory Work-ins', *New Society*, 22 August 1974]

Four of these occupations resulted in the creation of worker co-operatives. The first occurred at Fakenham in Norfolk in 1972: after a seventeen-week work-in a small group of women leather-workers managed to secure financial backing from the Scott Bader Commonwealth, a well-established co-operative organisation based on a successful co-ownership chemical company. The resulting Fakenham Enterprises remained a small-scale venture and at one point the workforce fell to eight workers. The survival of the organisation seemed to be assured, at least in the short term, when the Government announced in 1976 it was giving the co-operative £50,000 under the job creation programme to expand and give employment to an additional twenty-four people. Unfortunately this proved insufficient and the organisation ceased trading the following year.

The Kirkby Manufacturing and Engineering Co-operative is based on a single large factory near Liverpool. The factory had changed hands several times during the early 1970s and was the site of a sit-in in 1972. In June 1974 International Property Developers, the current owners, announced that the works would be closed and 1200 redundancies would result; at this time the factory was producing a diverse product line including soft drinks, panel radiators, electric storage heaters and also undertaking miscellaneous metal presswork jobs. When a receiver was appointed in the following month to liquidate the assets the workers escorted him to the gate and took control of the factory themselves. In November 1974, Tony Benn, Secretary of State for Industry in the Labour Government, announced that he had agreed in principle to provide the co-operative with £3·9 million in the form of a grant: about £1·8 million was paid immediately to the receiver for the factory equipment and stock.

The KME co-operative has continued to trade successfully, but the third co-operative had a shorter and less pleasant life. In March 1974 the Beaverbrook organisation announced the closure of printing operations in Glasgow, where the *Scottish Daily Express* was produced. Some 1800 jobs were in jeopardy and an Action Committee was established, eventually leading to a formation of a co-operative to produce a new paper, the *Scottish Daily News*. The workers' reaction was more practical than political; in the words of their Chairman: 'The entire history of the *Scottish Daily News* is founded in the determination of a group of trade union activists to fight against unemployment. Any other consideration was incidental.' [Allister Mackie, 'The Scottish Daily News', in *The New Worker Co-operatives* (Nottingham: Spokesman Books, 1976) p. 109]

The Government offered a loan of £1·75 million to the co-operative if the workers themselves could guarantee an equal sum. Eventually the money was raised through a combination of loans from trade unions, redundancy money from the co-operative members and a large individual contribution from Robert Maxwell, whose subsequent part in the co-operative's history was to cause considerable controversy. On 5 May 1975 the first edition of the *Scottish Daily News* was produced. The last edition appeared on 8 November in the same year. The workers' newspaper failed to secure and maintain the circulation that it needed to remain viable, despite the reduction in costs secured by higher productivity.

Since a defensive reaction to redundancy has been the major force behind the formation of the worker co-operatives, it is likely that they will be producing goods in markets which are declining or are highly competitive with low profit margins. If the market had been expanding and profitable the original firms would not have encountered any difficulties. The fourth co-operative, at Meriden, is producing a product, motor-cycles, where the factors that led to the decline of the British producers are only too evident. During the 1960s Japanese manufacturers entered the British market and came to dominate all segments of it. Faced with intensive competition, initially for the smaller ranges, British producers withdrew their models and eventually ended up making only the larger machines, with declining profitability.

What was evident in the home market was also happening abroad. Between 1968 and 1974 the UK market grew by 240 per cent but the British manufacturer's share fell from 34 per cent to 3 per cent; in North America the market grew by a similar amount and the British share fell from 11 per cent to 1 per cent. [Boston Consulting Group, *Strategy Alternatives for the British Motorcycle Industry* (London: HMSO, 1975)] Irrespective of the relative attractions of the competing machines, the Japanese manufacturers had secured price advantages which reflected much higher productivity: in 1975 Yamaha were producing 200 motor-cycles per man-year at their factory compared with 18 per man-year at the best British factory.

By 1973 the British industry had declined to three factories: BSA-Triumph owned Small Heath, in Birmingham, and Meriden; Norton Villiers owned Wolverhampton. In the summer of that year, BSA shares collapsed and their trading was suspended. The Conservative Government, two years on from 'lame ducks', sought to procure a merger between BSA and Norton with Denis Poore, formerly of Nortons, as Chairman. The dowry consisted of £4·8 million of Government money. Denis Poore announced his intention to close the Meriden factory whose main product was a well-known enthusiast's bike, the Triumph Bonneville. His justification for this choice was that the factory had never lived up to its potential and had experienced continued industrial relations difficulties.

Poore made his announcement in September 1973 and the workers immediately occupied the factory, shutting in £1 million worth of unfinished bikes. The commitment of the Meriden workers to the Bonneville bike was high; motor-cycles have a mystique which is missing from soft drinks, panel radiators and electric storage heaters. The workers knew that there was a continuing market for the Bonneville and gradually the idea of a co-operative evolved – in no small measure due to support from a number of Labour M.P.s and trade union officials.

Outside support for the venture became a possibility with the return of a Labour administration in February 1974. After a period of uncertainty, in part due to opposition from the other motor-cycle factories, in March 1975 the Government made a grant of £750,000 and a loan of £4·2 million to allow the workers to buy the Meriden plant from Norton Villiers Triumph. By this time most of the 1750 workers originally employed had left and the co-operative opened with a workforce of 300. Further support was needed at the beginning of 1977 when the co-operative received additional Government aid to enable them to purchase the marketing organisation and related assets. At the same time Sir Arnold Weinstock's electrical manufacturing conglomerate, GEC, loaned £1 million of working capital, which was repaid by the end of the year.

The organisation of the co-operative follows the Yugoslavian pattern: the Supervisory Board consists of eight shop-floor representatives elected through the trade union movement, two outside representatives and a Government nominee; underneath the Supervisory Board is a management board. With an organisation as small as the Meriden factory, and given the experience that the remaining workers had undergone, the organisational pattern is far less important than the part played by the personalities of the leaders. This is equally true of the other new producer co-operatives.

The most evident improvement under the new form of organisation has been in the area of labour relations. Within months of its formation the Meriden Chairman was able to boast that:

> At the moment with 360 workers, including office staff, we are turning out about 250 bikes a week. We plan to turn out 500 a week with about 750 people. In the old days at Triumph we were hard pushed to make 600 with 1750 people.

The quality of the work had also improved. 'In the old days some 80% of the output went straight into the rectification bay where twenty people were working. Now we have only five there.' Part of the success could be attributed to the increased flexibility brought about by the absence of differentials. With very limited exceptions all employees received the same weekly wage packet; this was originally set at £50, well below comparable rates in neighbouring factories. Currently a productivity bonus scheme is under discussion.

Opposition to the Government's support of the co-operative came from a variety of sources, but one area deserves particular consideration. Tony Benn, at the Department of Industry, intimated that initial aid to Meriden would be dependent on acquiescence elsewhere in the industry. In November 1974 Benn paid a hurried trip to the Birmingham Small Heath factory in an attempt to persuade the 1200 workers there that the co-operative did not directly threaten their jobs. It had been Denis Poore's intention to concentrate Triumph production at Small Heath after closing Meriden. Two months later a mass meeting of the Small Heath workers agreed to remove their veto on Meriden on the assurance that immediate talks would take place between unions, the Norton Villiers management and the Government on the future of the

British motor-cycle industry as a whole.

The subsequent history of the Small Heath and Wolverhampton factories makes disturbing reading. Denis Poore had already expressed his view that a three-factory industry would require substantially greater investment and the Government commissioned an independent review of the industry from the Boston Consulting Group. This report, which was released in July 1975, set out the background of the industry's decline and considered a number of alternative strategies for the future. Tony Benn's successor at the Department of Industry, Eric Varley, announced that the Government had looked at all the alternatives and found that none of them were viable, so no further Government aid would be made available for Norton Villiers. Denis Poore described the decision as showing 'a callous disregard for the effect on the livelihood of thousands of men and for solemn assurances given by Mr Benn when he persuaded the workforce to go along with his plan for expanding the industry to three factories'.

Shortly afterwards Norton Villiers announced that it intended to place its subsidiary which owned and operated the Wolverhampton factory into liquidation and concentrate on limited production at Small Heath. The Wolverhampton workers then began a factory blockade themselves, which continued throughout a whole series of abortive negotiations for the factory. At the end of 1975 manufacturing ceased at Small Heath and the factory was also placed in receivership. Apart from a small Norton Villiers operation at Lichfield assembling mopeds, Meriden became the sole survivor of the British motor-cycle industry.

In the examples considered in this chapter, at Fakenham, KME, the *Scottish Daily News* and Meriden, a combination of special circumstances enabled the idea of co-operation to take root. There is, however, a case for worker co-operation as a more general ingredient of industrial policy.

Self-organisation can make work more meaningful and bring fulfilment through greater participation. The degree of commitment from the members of the co-operatives has been considerable; workers have been prepared to invest savings and redundancy money in ventures from which there was little prospect of short-term return. In the case of the *Scottish Daily News* the resulting losses were tragic.

Each of the new co-operatives started as a defensive reaction against unemployment; any commitment to the co-operative ideal appeared later. The move towards co-operatives did not spring from any concerted political theory. All were led by strong and forceful personalities, particularly within the trade union movement at the factories. This explains why the idea of a co-operative gained acceptance at Meriden and not at the other two motor-cycle

factories. Government support for the Meriden venture was justified
by the determination that the workers themselves displayed in fight-
ing for the new form of organisation.

There is, however, no cause for starry-eyed idealism and it is
totally unrealistic at this time to argue for an industrial policy
based entirely on worker co-operatives. Co-operatives cannot sur-
vive without extensive external finance which must come from the
Government. The Rochdale Pioneers were able to build up their
movement from their own savings and ploughed-back profits; it
would be impossible to do this in today's capital-intensive society.
Another problem that will face the co-operatives is the role of professional management. Meriden was aided by management teams
from Guest, Keen & Nettlefolds and the General Electric Company
(GEC). If expertise is to be hired from outside, a number of questions on the salary to be paid and eligibility for co-operative membership will need to be resolved. There is no guarantee that further
co-operatives will be as fortunate in their leadership as KME and
Meriden.

All these difficulties point to the need for a clear Government
policy on worker co-operatives. The Government money that has
been made available was provided on the basis of the need to support worthwhile experiments. Criticism of the Government's stand
came from the Industrial Development Advisory Board, a body set
up to advise the Department on company applications for State
aid, and the public Accounts Committee of the House of Commons.
The Advisory Board's annual commentary argued that:

> The Board sympathises with and respects the aspirations of those
> working in an enterprise to see it continue and shoulder greater
> responsibility for its operation. However, to attempt to introduce
> the co-operative approach in concerns which have collapsed in a
> sharply competitive market, and where prospects of viability are
> remote, is not, in the Board's view, a propitious way to support
> these aspirations.

In the first few months of 1977 Parliament considered and passed
the Industrial Common Ownership Act, which commits the Government to providing £400,000 over the next five years to assist the
development of co-operative ventures. Considering the sums of
money required by the co-operatives discussed above, the new Act
is scarcely likely to have a great deal of impact. As an expression of
the Government's determination to see co-operative ventures continue, it is, however, important. What is urgently needed is not
just finance but a clear statement of the circumstances where a co-
operative is likely to qualify for support.

The development of co-operation should not be concentrated

exclusively in markets which are declining or with low profit margins – where survival is so difficult. Determination is a necessary condition for the survival of a co-operative, but by itself it is insufficient.

5 Dilemmas of Public Ownership

There was a tragi-comic aspect to Shinwell's introduction to the job. When instructed by Attlee to nationalise the mines, he inquired at Transport House for the products of Labour thinking over the years. After all, this was not a new subject. Coal nationalisation had been on Labour's programme for a quarter of a century. Somebody must have worked something out at some time. The archives were ransacked and revealed two copies of a paper written by Jim Griffiths, one of them a translation into Welsh.

[Lord Wigg, *George Wigg*]

One lesson to be learned from the case studies presented in the previous chapter, especially the discussion on the steel industry, is that a demand for nationalisation by itself cannot constitute a complete industrial policy. However strong the case for public ownership, practical problems remain to be solved once an industry is nationalised. If these problems are not recognised and a transfer in ownership is seen as the complete answer, disillusionment with the performance of public ownership will inevitably result.

This chapter will attempt to expose some of the areas of difficulty that must be considered if public ownership is to achieve its potential. The industries cannot be socialised unless these underlying conflicts and contradictions are taken into account. Five particular problems will be considered: the underlying purpose of industry, the objectives that follow from the purpose chosen, the difficulties of satisfying consumers, the trade-off between efficiency and redundancy, and the role of professional management. The first four problems are closely linked, while the fifth is quite separate.

WHO SHOULD INDUSTRY SERVE?

'Who should industry serve?' calls into question the whole objective of the industrial system. It is rarely asked explicitly and, when asked, the issue is generally sidestepped by an answer which refers to some vague concept of the 'public good'. This can come equally from advocates of systems based on public or private ownership. This section seeks to expose some of the problems underlying such conceptions of the public good and these will be illustrated by a consideration of the current debate on private ownership.

One qualification should be made in advance. The industrial system is a system in the full technical sense of the word: it amounts in total to more than the sum of the individual parts. When discussing the purpose of industry it is important to recognise that we are generally considering the industrial system as a whole. What the aim or purpose of an industrial system should be is a subtly but significantly different question from what the objective of an individual industrial enterprise should be.

Supporters of public ownership often find it difficult to state what the objective of the industrial system as a whole should be, in part because of the tendency to confuse the creation of an economic surplus with the profit motive. An industrial system is needed to take inputs, process them and produce an output that society values more than the sum of the separate inputs. This is no more a capitalist view of industry than it is a socialist one. Socialist objections to the private ownership system stem from observations about the nature of the surplus: in particular that measuring the surplus in terms of the profitability of individual firms is harmful and that the ultimate distribution of the surplus is wrong.

In classical economics the objective of each individual firm is profit-maximisation. If the firm pursues its objective, and investors and workers play their part, the best allocation of resources will be achieved and overall welfare maximised. The behaviour of private enterprise in practice will be considered in a later chapter, but at this stage it should be recognised that its theoretical basis in welfare economics is tenuous to say the least. In particular, 'externalities', the incidental costs and benefits for which no charge is made, and the effect of different distributions of income are ignored.

The legal obligations of private companies have always reflected the assumptions of classical welfare economics. Company law – much of which is case law – is based on the rights of the shareholders. Shareholders alone can draw up and amend the memorandum and articles of association which state what the company can do and set out its internal organisation. It is recognised that in practice shareholders will delegate much of this responsibility to directors, who have a duty to act in the best interests of the company. A classic test case, *Parke v. The Daily News Limited,* occurred in 1962 and the result was described in the following terms:

> The Cadbury family, who controlled the selling company, wished to distribute the whole of the purchase price among the employees who would become redundant. At the suit of one shareholder they were restrained from doing so. To the argument that 'the prime duty must be to the shareholders; but boards of directors must take into consideration their duties to employees in these days', Plowman J. answered tersely 'but no authority to support

that proposition as a proposition of law was cited to me; I know of none and in my judgement such is not the law.'

[L. C. B. Gower, *The Principles of Modern Company Law* (London: Stevens & Sons, 1969) pp. 522–3]

The argument that directors of private companies should take into consideration their duties to employees, and also those to consumers and the community, has gained momentum in recent years. In March 1972 the Confederation of British Industry set up a Working Party to inquire into industrial management, which reported eighteen months later. The report, published as *The Responsibilities of the British Public Company: Final Report of the Company Affairs Committee*, unsurprisingly endorsed the principle of the private enterprise system and the profit motive. More positively it called for a general legislative encouragement for companies 'to recognise duties and obligations (within the context of the objects for which the company was established) arising from the company's relationships with creditors, suppliers, customers, employees and society at large'. In the absence of legislative support the Working Party recommended that directors adhere to a number of principles of corporate conduct.

This recognition of the interests of groups other than shareholders was central to the on-going debate about the socially responsible company. The groups have become known as 'stakeholders' and the three categories considered most important are, employees, customers, and the public interest. Three years later a survey of 130 companies undertaken by the British Institute of Management concluded that there was wide support for the introduction of a written code of conduct to recognise these stake-holder interests.

Much of the discussion on the socially responsible company was prompted by growing criticism of the behaviour of the private sector. The Confederation of British Industry's response was to try and alter marginally the stated objectives of industrial enterprises, without considering the implications for the rationale of the private ownership system as a whole. The way in which the concept of the socially responsible individual company struck at the heart of the doctrine of private enterprise was, however, recognised by one of the system's most articulate advocates, Milton Friedman, who argued that 'few trends could so thoroughly undermine the very foundations of our free society as the acceptance by corporate officials of a social responsibility other than to make as much for their shareholders as possible'. [Milton Friedman, *Capitalism and Freedom* (Chicago: University of Chicago Press, 1962) p. 133] The recognition of the interests of stake-holders by the supporters of private enterprise amounted, as Friedman pointed out, to a loss of nerve and loss of faith in the capacity of the system as a whole to achieve its objective.

The interests of stake-holders must be taken into account whatever pattern of industrial ownership is adopted. The recognition of this problem in discussions on public sector organisation has been limited, though the debate on the implications of industrial democracy has led to similar considerations. In a written answer to a Parliamentary Question in 1976 on progress towards industrial democracy in the public sector, the Minister for the Civil Service, Charles Morris, replied that:

> Industrial democracy in the public sector presents special problems because of the role of Parliament and local authorities as representatives of the electorate and, so far as the nationalised industries are concerned, because of the ultimate responsibility of sponsoring Ministers to Parliament. It is fundamental to the working of democracy as we know it that elected representatives take decisions and act in the interests of the community as a whole: that principle cannot be breached. But, within the need to preserve the accountability of elected representatives and the requirements of the public interest, employees and the representatives in the public services should be given the maximum opportunity to contribute their views on matters of legitimate staff interest.
>
> [*Hansard*, 11 February 1976, cols 240–1]

This answer raises some important questions, not just on the organisation of individual industries, but on the operation of public ownership as a system. Charles Morris argued that nationalised industries must seek to achieve the objectives set down by elected representatives 'in the interests of the community as a whole'. The direct interests of the workers and, by implication, other groups of stake-holders must be a secondary consideration.

It is important to distinguish between laying down objectives from above and allowing them to result from the interaction of the various stake-holder groups. This distinction underlies many of the arguments advanced later in this book. At this stage it is enough to draw attention to the problem. Advocates of any system of industrial ownership must find a way of ensuring that an economic surplus is achieved without exploiting stake-holder interests. The organisation of each individual enterprise must be seen in relation to this purpose.

WHAT SORT OF OBJECTIVES?

Clearly the objectives for an individual enterprise should follow from the purpose of the industrial system as a whole. In the previous section this was defined as the creation of an economic surplus, but it should not be inferred that each enterprise must itself create the maximum surplus with the resources that it can obtain. One of the traditional arguments advanced for public ownership is that capitalism, by allowing each individual firm to profit-maximise, reduces the level of the overall surplus; a greater surplus will be created and it will be better distributed if other objectives are set for each enterprise. Since narrow profit-based criteria are rejected these new objectives should have social, as well as financial, content. This section concentrates on the problems of developing objectives which can measure performance in terms other than profitability.

Chapter 2 described those objectives which have been set for the nationalised industries since the war. The only important development of the instruction that the industries should ensure that revenues are not less than sufficient to meet all charges properly chargeable to revenue account, taking one year with another, was the introduction of financial targets in the 1961 White Paper. The limitations of financial targets are now recognised. It would, therefore, seem likely that an attempt to control publicly-owned industry by considering performances against orthodox financial yardsticks alone is unlikely to be successful. If other yardsticks are introduced, however, they must be accepted by all parties involved and give a clear practical measure of the industry's performance. One of the most powerful arguments for the use of financial measures of performance is that they are generally regarded as objective. In fact accountancy is as much an art as a science and the recent debate on inflation accounting demonstrates the difficulty in attempting to measure economic surplus by orthodox methods.

Some broader objectives were implied in the statutes that established the nationalised industries. The Electricity Boards were required to extend electricity to rural areas; the various Transport Acts imposed complex obligations on the constituent industries. However, these objectives have never been supported by a method of measurement and the ambiguities have remained. This has caused concern in the industries themselves. The 1976 NEDO report stated that all public corporation boards saw themselves as performing a primarily commercial role within the constraints of maintaining security of supply and standards of service which satisfied reasonable demand. The report went on to argue that confusion over social obligations was one of the main causes of the sour relationship between the boards and the Government.

The transport industries have been particularly vulnerable to the problem of inadequately expressed objectives and successive Chairmen of British Rail have not hesitated to point forcefully to the need for a new approach. Richard Marsh has argued that, if you take British Rail in isolation:

> It could be said that all these services should be run on a strictly commercial basis to maximise the profit: but, of course, if we were to pursue that policy to its logical end, we would probably shut all of the commuter services into London, and that would clearly be nonsense. Alternatively, it could be argued that the task of the railway management should be to shift the maximum amount of freight from road to rail: that sounds good; but that policy, if it were carried to extremes, could involve a massive and a quite unrealistic bill for the taxpayer. Again, you could argue that freight on the railway should be carried on strict commercial criteria; yet even that might well conflict with Government policies in developing districts, where vast sums of public money are being poured in, in the hope of attracting industrial development. This means that, far too frequently, the public sector manager, in the absence of clear objectives, has to maintain a very sensitive ear to public and political opinion and define the objectives himself as he goes along.
>
> [Richard Marsh, in *Managing to Survive* (London: BBC Publications, 1975) p. 15]

Marsh's successor, Peter Parker, called for the creation of a contract with the Government to state quite clearly the agreed price for services and for performances year by year to be measured against this contract.

Another call for a new approach to objectives has come from the National Consumer Council which advocated the establishment of consumer objectives as standards against which the performance of nationalised industries could properly be measured. The Consumer Council recommended that they should be drawn up by individual consumer councils:

> embracing large objectives as well as small, from the size of the rail or bus network down to standards for punctuality by which the service in one year can be compared with that in another; from the rate of expansion in telecommunications down to the minimum tolerable limits for the proportion of wrong numbers obtained; from the continuity of supplies of energy down to the tolerable delays there should be in obtaining spare parts for, and doing repairs to, gas and electric appliances.
>
> [National Consumer Council, *Consumers and the Nationalised Industries* (London: HMSO, 1976) pp. 79–80]

The development of social and consumer objectives is of great importance to advocates of socialised public industry. If the profit motive is seen to be a hindrance to the creation of an economic surplus, because of its failure to take all costs and benefits into account, other yardsticks are essential. Yet there has been scarcely any debate at all on the way that they could be derived and on what form they could take.

One possible method of tackling the problem was set out in the 1976 NEDO report. One of the tasks that would be delegated to the Policy Council, whose establishment was recommended in the study, was the agreement and publication of criteria and targets appropriate to the industry. The report by Cooper and Lybrand Associates, as part of the study, went a stage further and recommended the creation of a guidelines package for each individual industry. Included amongst the guidelines would be a specified minimum level of service and the acceptance of certain social obligations as well as the more orthodox financial targets. Much of the inspiration for this approach came from a study of current practice in France. In 1967 a Working Party, chaired by M. Simon Nora, investigated publicly-owned industry and recommended the negotiation of 'contrats-de-programme'. Only two contracts have, however, been successfully negotiated, for the electricity and railway corporations.

There are three questions involved in the establishment of social or commercial objectives: what form should they take?; who should set them?; how are they to be monitored? The first and second questions are interrelated. If the objectives are set as a result of an agreement between the various stake-holders involved – presumably workers, Government, consumers and management – they will take the form acceptable to all bodies. The form of monitoring required raises important problems posed by the defensive attitude shown by the public corporations towards the provision of information.

The need for secrecy is sometimes dictated by legitimate reasons, for example when the dissemination of information can lead to collusion on the part of suppliers, when overseas competitors can take commercial advantage, when defence commitments or internal staff matters are involved. The amount of secrecy needed for these reasons is however greatly overstated and this is true of the whole process of Government in Britain. The USA, by contrast, introduced a 'Freedom of Information Act' as long ago as 1966 which gives ordinary citizens the right to request from any agency of the Federal Government whatever public records interest them. If the Government agency chooses to, it can invoke one of the nine exemptions to deny the information, but these exemptions are not mandatory.

The deterioration in the information contained in the current annual reports of the public corporations is a sign of this trend towards greater secrecy. Annual reports have become increasingly more attractively produced, and more expensive, and contain less useful information. It is very difficult to extract such useful figures as labour productivity from some industry reports. Much more statistical information used to be published about detailed operations by the old railway companies than is currently offered by British Rail. If new forms of objectives are to have any validity, attitudes towards the provision of information must alter.

THE ROLE OF THE CONSUMER

The most powerfully argued case against the form of industrial democracy advocated by the Trades Union Congress has come from the National Consumer Council. Their argument is based on the premise that the TUC proposals will lead to collusion between labour and capital which will work to the detriment of the consumer. Historically, it has often been argued that consumers are the most important external stake-holders in the industrial system: Sidney and Beatrice Webb in their *A Constitution for the Socialist Commonwealth of Great Britain* (London: London School of Economics, 1920) suggested that consumers, employees and managements should each have one-third of the membership of nationalised industry boards. It has also been accepted that public ownership needs to be particularly responsive to consumer needs because of the monopolistic nature of the industries. The supply of electric lighting and postal services, for example, are almost complete monopolies; if the consumer is not able to take his custom elsewhere, it is important that he should be satisfied with the service offered.

When the post-war industries were established it was thought at first that the public corporation structure would itself be sufficient to ensure that the consumer interest was considered. The mechanism for consumer representation was added as an afterthought. There was little interest in the problem inside the sponsoring Ministries and an internal memorandum specifically stated that 'where an industry is in the hands of a Public Board, however, no conflict can arise between the interests of shareholders and of consumers (except where, as in the case of LPTB "C" Stock, there is variable interest stock'. [Sir Norman Chester, *The Nationalisation of British Industry 1945–51* (London: HMSO, 1975) pp. 642–3] As a result of pressure from the Parliamentary Committee considering the Coal Bill, the Government later decided to establish Domestic and Industrial Coal Consumers Councils, and these provided the model for the other nationalised industries.

The Domestic Coal Consumers Council had the duty of considering any matters affecting the sale or supply of coal for domestic consumption. It was supplied with a small secretariat by the Minister who appointed its members. Other councils had the similar function of straddling the divide between consumer and industry, but the title and form of organisation varied. Some industries were given 'consultative committees', rather than 'consumer councils', some industries had regional committees as well as national committees.

From this haphazard beginning the councils have survived, almost unaltered, to this present day – despite a succession of inquiries which were without exception critical of their limited role. In 1968 the Consumer Council issued a report which, though it concluded that the councils were doing useful work, called for a series of changes in their organisation. It recommended that the council offices should be separated from those of the Boards, and placed accessibly, and that the councils should be independently financed.

The 1970–1 Report from the Select Committee on Nationalised Industries, *Relations with the Public*, also advocated greater separation of the councils from the industries. It put the case for the councils having far greater expertise made available to them, though this should not take the form of permanent expert staff. Both studies pointed out that the general public was insufficiently aware of the existence of the councils. This view was confirmed in a 1974 Report undertaken for the Consumers' Association, and published in *Which*. This showed that only 21 per cent of Consumers' Association members and 8 per cent of the general public had ever heard of the Gas Consumers Council.

The most comprehensive survey into the activities of the councils was that published by the National Consumer Council in 1976. This concluded that the proportion of the general public who were aware of consumer councils had in fact fallen during the previous ten years. Equally disturbing, only a very small proportion of those with unsolved complaints referred them to councils; the proportion was thought to be highest in relation to the gas industry at about one in twenty.

The processing of complaints is only one aspect of the consumer interest and the NCC Report was depressing about the other main aspects:

Our surveys showed considerable concern about this – a general feeling that nationalised industries are not doing a very good job in providing value for money, that their standards of service have declined, and that consumers have a right to be consulted about how they should operate.

[National Consumer Council, *Consumers and the Nationalised Industries* (London: HMSO, 1976) p. 53]

The councils appear to have had so little power over 'policy formulation' especially and above all on prices. This is for consumers the salient fact about the nationalised industries in the last year or so. Prices have been soaring upwards, and the bevy of councils seems to many uncharitable onlookers to have been standing by, watching, deploring, saying the right things but failing to do anything. They have not in short been the sort of shield that most consumers would have liked them to be.   [p. 78]

The NCC considered but did not recommend the abolition of the councils. It supported strengthening the councils in a variety of ways: by insisting that any change in tariffs should be referred to the councils in advance; by placing council Chairmen automatically on the industry boards; appointing other consumer representatives to Boards; and by housing the national councils together so that some joint expertise could be developed.

The council generally considered to have been the most successful is the Post Office Users' National Council which the Post Office has a statutory duty to consult on major changes. Since 1973 POUNC, in common with all other councils, has its thirty-three members appointed by the Secretary of State for Prices and Consumer Protection; it has a full-time staff of sixteen. It has secured a number of minor successes in obtaining clearer telephone bills and the relaxation of a clause disclaiming Post Office liability in its GIRO agreements. Its most important success occurred in 1976 when it persuaded the Government to establish the independent Carter Committee to undertake a fundamental review of the industry. However, the limited powers of the council were demonstrated when it asked the Post Office for estimates of the revenue effects of two increases in the charge for sending parcels and was refused the information on the grounds that the figures were 'commercially confidential'.

Many of the issues taken up by the other councils seem depressingly trivial. The Central Transport Consultative Council entered into a running dispute with British Rail on dirty uniforms in restaurant cars, untidy buffet cars and wet and dirty table-tops. It later fought a successful campaign against British Rail's decision to cease carrying unaccompanied livestock – to the relief of pigeon-fanciers. The National Gas Consumers' Council did not hear of the Chancellor's decision to increase gas prices by up to a tenth until his 1976 mini-budget speech was reported in the following day's papers.

Most of the studies cited have supported the existence of consumer councils and called for them to be strengthened in one way or another; but there has been little discussion on the underlying relationship between the consumers and the industry, apart from a consideration of ways of processing complaints. One of the difficulties in developing a policy for consumer representation is the absence of a clearly identifiable consumer constituency. In some industries the larger consumers are quite able to take care of themselves – the Central Electricity Generating Board is the Coal Board's biggest customer. The consumer movement has been growing in importance since the establishment of the Consumers' Association in 1957 but its views have been expressed with a marked middle-class accent. When considering eligibility for appointment to consumer councils the National Consumer Council was forced to fall back on the circular recommendation that:

> Anyone being a consumer should be eligible provided only that he or she has ability, willingness to put in some hard work and capacity to look at problems of industrial policy from the point of view of the people whom every industry exists (or should exist) to serve.   [*Consumers and the Nationalised Industries*, p. 110]

The appointment of directors charged with representing the consumer interest is one proposal aimed at improving the nationalised industries' relationships with their customers. Two other suggestions deserve some consideration. Justice, an independent organisation of lawyers, has suggested the creation of a consumers' Ombudsman to investigate and report on cases where the complainant was not satisfied with the outcome of a consumer council's action or with the response of the nationalised industry itself. Ken Coates, a leading theorist for the Institute for Workers' Control, has suggested a new approach based on a recognition of separation of powers. Direct representation, he argued, is impossible so the consumer needs access to objective information and the means to contribute his own information to the stock of such knowledge; the repository for such information should be rigorously separate from the industries but should have inviolable rights to access to relevant facts.

This last approach is attractive but the difficulties in obtaining objective information should not be underestimated. Tony Benn, when appointed Secretary for Energy, tried to ensure that the consumer information put out by the different fuel industries was harmonised. Eventually the Department produced a booklet called *Compare Your Home Heating Costs* which set out tables showing the costs of buying and running different kinds of heating equipment using different fuels. Gas was shown to have a comparative advantage and the electricity industry reacted angrily; many local chairmen refused to allow their showrooms to stock the booklet. If the Department of Energy could not obtain agreement in the face of industry chauvinism what hope would there be for an independent consumers' organisation?

EFFICIENCY AND REDUNDANCY

Whatever form of industrial system is adopted it is evident that the consumer's interest will be best served if it is operated in the most efficient manner and costs are kept to a minimum. In economic theory two sorts of efficiency are generally identified: allocative and internal efficiency. Allocative efficiency relates to the division of resources between the different enterprises; internal efficiency relates to the control of resources within the individual enterprise. Many economists have argued that the amount to be gained by increased allocative efficiency is trivial compared to the amount to be gained by increased internal efficiency.

This theoretical viewpoint appears to be reflected in popular public attitudes towards the nationalised industries. The general impression held is that the public corporations are, in common with most Governmental organisations, bumbling and inefficient bureaucracies. This view is generally based on misapprehensions and prejudice rather than on the available evidence, but that does not make it any less of a problem to supporters of public ownership. The American economist, J. K. Galbraith, has never missed an opportunity to remind the European left of this fact of life:

> This sector, to state what is obvious but often avoided, must be administered at the highest level of efficiency and competence. No argument against public ownership is so effective as the allegation that it is incompetent. Nothing so affirms people in mistrust of public ownership as their own discovery that this is so.
> ['Economic Problems of the Left', *New Statesman*, 20 February 1976, p. 218]

The biggest criticism of the performance of public ownership has generally been concerned with real or supposed overmanning. Alleged overmanning causes offence because of its arbitrary nature. Why, it is argued, should employees in nationalised industries be cushioned from the worst effects of economic recession while those who have the misfortune to work in the private sector are made redundant? This argument is unfair. One of the real areas of success of public ownership has been, ironically, in shedding manpower. Far from maintaining a steady labour force the basic public sector industries have supervised a sustained orderly rundown in the labour force.

Nevertheless, some nationalised industries have recently come in for harsh criticism, and British Rail provides the outstanding example. The First Report of the Select Committee on Nationalised Industries, session 1976–7, on *The Role of British Rail in Public Transport* considered railway manpower and argued that British

Rail had the lowest productivity of the main north-west European railway systems. Other railways had experienced increases in traffic with stable labour forces.

The Select Committee recommended that the number of 'second men' carried in cabs should be reduced to at most 2000, consisting only of men needed for training and promotion. This proposal was supported by a number of independent studies. Railway Rescue, a voluntary group of enthusiasts, in their evidence to the Committee, suggested that there were something like 32,000 surplus drivers, guards and administrators and, in particular, 'the job the guard performs on many, though not all, trains is an anachronism.' A highly critical book, published two years earlier, argued that:

> Second men are almost completely unnecessary, except in the case of those diesel passenger trains where the carriages are steam-heated and the second man looks after the boiler. However, British Rail is planning to eliminate these boilers by 1977. None of the other arguments which might be used to justify the presence of second men have any substance. They are not there to take over the controls in order to relieve the driver because they are not required to be qualified drivers. . . . That second men are not required is shown by the fact that they have already been eliminated in a number of other countries, including Switzerland, Austria and, for electric passenger trains, Norway.
>
> [Richard Pryke and John Dodgson, *The Rail Problem* (London: Martin Robertson, 1975) p. 145]

The Pryke and Dodgson study suggested that, by a combination of measures, British Rail's manpower might be reduced from 225,000 in 1974 to 153,000 by 1981 without any increase in capital expenditure. Their conclusions were attacked by both management and unions. The main counter-argument was that over the previous decade the labour force had been cut from 475,000 to 255,000. There is, though it was not explicitly stated, a limit to the rate of rundown; any further contraction above that planned by British Rail would jeopardise the future role that the railways could play in transport policy.

Not one of British Rail's critics faced up to the central problem. Even if the overmanning argument was demonstrated to be true beyond any reasonable doubt, the problem of adjustment would remain. The rundown of surplus manpower is not easy to achieve in the face of trade union opposition – and the trade union is only fulfilling its function by questioning such proposals. This problem is particularly severe in the case where production is concentrated in a small number of geographical areas as was shown in the previous discussion on the modernisation of the steel industry in Wales.

The difficulties are an inevitable result of attempts to capture economies of scale by increasing the average size of the production unit. That this can happen under private as well as public industry was demonstrated in the case of the collapse of Rolls-Royce.

One of the biggest areas of failure in the performance of public ownership has been the absence of specific policies to deal with these problems. Special social payments have been made to both the National Coal Board and the Electricity Generating Board to avoid the worst effects of the rundown in colliery manpower. These have, however, served to cause confusion in the financial accountability of the industries concerned. One imaginative new response over the last decade has been the establishment of BSC (Industries) Ltd to deal with the worst effects of closure in the steel industries. Although the organisation only operates on a comparatively small scale, with an annual budget of about £5·6 million, it has been given a great deal of internal importance inside the British Steel Corporation. The BSC Chairman, Sir Charles Villiers, has taken over control of BSC (Industries) and attempts to bring new employment into closure areas have met with some limited success. About 980 new jobs have been created in Ebbw Vale since 1972, with prospects of another 1800 over the next four years, by a combination of financial incentives and drawing attention to the 'reliable and flexible work-force' which is available.

The conflict between efficiency and redundancy is likely to continue to be of critical importance and an honest recognition of its existence is the first step towards its resolution. There is no evidence that the public ownership of industry will, of itself, guarantee the maximum use of the economic resources available and full employment. It is always possible to inflate the labour force and introduce concealed unemployment, but this is an evasion rather than a solution of the problem. Moreover, deliberate policies to create artificial employment levels can hinder the movement to economically useful jobs when they become available.

Part of the difficulty is allegedly caused by the workers' resistance to change – though there is very little evidence of this existing as a general reaction in the nationalised industries. Those who do identify and criticise the pockets of opposition to redundancy that do exist should consider one important fact: most industrial workers are deeply aware of the marked deterioration in economic and social status which would result from unemployment. While the gap between the standard of living of those who are in and those who are out of work is so great, defensive attitudes are scarcely surprising. A new attitude and the development of an employment policy are therefore essential for the efficient working of a public ownership system.

THE ROLE OF PROFESSIONAL MANAGEMENT

Emanuel Shinwell, replying to the debate on public ownership held at the 1945 Labour Party Conference, proclaimed:

> Let us not confuse private enterprise with individual enterprise, the enterprise of our technicians, our scientists, our inventors, of whom many are now in the ranks of the Labour Party and ready to place their services at our disposal. The Labour Party and the next Labour Government will seek to encourage the scientist, the technician and the inventor to ask of them that they shall place their services at the disposal of the State for public good and not for private gain, and we are satisfied there will be a ready and generous response.
>
> [LPACR (Blackpool), 1945, p. 137]

The thirty years that have passed since this optimistic note was struck have witnessed growing disillusionment amongst those whose expertise has been 'placed at the disposal of the State'. Two particular manifestations have been evident. First, the relationships between the sponsoring Ministers and the Board Members of the public corporations have deteriorated, certainly since the mid-1970s, so that public disputes are now a frequent occurrence. Secondly, the failure of public sector management to develop a particular ethos or style has resulted in their being chosen, unfairly, as suitable scapegoats by some sections in the Labour Movement.

The most open public row between a Chairman of a nationalised industry and a Government Minister took place between Sir Monty Finniston of the British Steel Corporation and Tony Benn and has already been outlined in an earlier chapter. The other disputes have tended to be less direct and personal, with the industry Chairman challenging the method of control of public industry rather than the Minister himself. Sir Arthur Hawkins, Chairman of the Central Electricity Generating Board until 1977, after resisting an open instruction from Tony Benn (then at the Department of Energy) to order the controversial Drax 'B' power station, marked his retirement press conference with an attack on the 'meddling' Civil Service and continued by arguing that:

> Flagrant attempts have been made, for short-term political ends, to pull the rug from under our feet. But we are not lap-dogs to be turned this way and that way. We have stood firm. This has not increased our popularity in Whitehall, but no one has succeeded in making us take a single step which, in my view, was against the interests of the industry and its consumers.

It was a response to 'meddling', in part, that had led to the formation of the Nationalised Industries Chairmen's Group in 1975.
Eighteen major public corporations were represented at the in-
augural press conference and Sir William Ryland of the Post Office
was chosen as the Group's first Chairman. One item was evidently
high on the agenda: the growing discontent about the freeze on
the salaries of nationalised industry Board members. The Board
members had a strong case to make. According to a study undertaken by Incomes Data Services Ltd, their salaries had been halved
in real terms over the five years to 1977. At the beginning of 1972
Board members' pay was set at the level recommended by the Top
Salaries Review Board, under the chairmanship of Lord Boyle; the
increases proposed for 1974 in the same review were not implemented and no alternative proposals were put forward. Matters
came to a head when five directors of Cable and Wireless Ltd, one
of the least known nationalised industries, threatened to resign *en
bloc* at the 1976 Annual Meeting.

The Chairman of Cable and Wireless was paid £12,828 a year
at the time; in addition he was given a company car and the option
of membership of a private health insurance scheme. In comparison
with the salary received by executives doing similar jobs in comparable industries his pay was inadequate; in comparison with the
wages received by the vast majority of workers in nationalised industries his pay was ample. What has been lacking, as the treatment
of the Top Salaries Review Board recommendations demonstrates,
is a clear policy for the status and payment of public sector management which can enable these and similar dilemmas to be resolved.

The way that the Board members of the major public corporations are chosen is another example of the absence of a coherent
attitude. Despite attempts by some Ministers, particularly Tony
Benn, to open out the whole process, the system of appointments
is shrouded in secrecy. A Public Appointments Unit operates within
the Civil Service with:

> Ten full-time civil servants, of whom five are clerical and secre-
> tarial staff. The Unit's primary purpose is to identify the widest
> possible cross-section of people, from all parts of the country, able
> to undertake public work. Details of such people are made avail-
> able as required, to Departments whose Ministers make appoint-
> ments to public boards.

Apart from this bald information, given in answer to a Parliamentary Question of 5 May 1977, almost nothing is known about
the list of 'the Great and the Good'. Public advertisement procedures are used very rarely for filling public corporation board posts
and the only board-level posts that had been advertised in the

previous five years were in the Scottish Development Agency.

Political supporters of public ownership have always found it difficult to face up to the problems posed by the existence of professional management. Consequently the distinction between professional competence and commitment to public ownership has been a source of loose thinking. Discussions on the industries at local Labour Party meetings do not get far before someone declares that all would be well if all the managers were socialists. Since, in common with about half the population, some are not, they make convenient scapegoats for the shortcomings of the industries. Consider this extract from the 1975 Labour Party Conference. The speaker was a Tribune MP:

> The performance of certain of our existing publicly-owned industries leaves very much to be desired. I have a constituency interest in steel. It is, perhaps, the most bureaucratic of all our publicly-owned industries, with the most inept management it is possible to imagine [applause]. The overall direction of the industry is devoid of imagination; hordes of bureaucrats plotting redundancies for thousands of workers. Perhaps there should be redundancies in the Steel Industry but they should start at the top with these people [applause].
>
> [LPACR (Blackpool), 1975, p. 225]

The previous chapter drew attention to the absence of a clear policy for the steel industry and, although steel industry management has been maladroit, to attack them in this way is unfair. That it should strike a responsive chord at a Labour Party Conference is disturbing. Unfortunately management has historically been associated with ownership in Britain and historic class resentments have spilled over to the newer professional management in the nationalised industries. There are two misconceptions which need to be thoroughly exposed before a new attitude to public sector management can be developed. First, industrial democracy means that there is no need for management at all. Secondly, all managers should be ideologically committed to public ownership.

The extent to which orthodox management is compatible with industrial democracy will be considered in the following chapter. Whatever system of participation is adopted, however, there will be need for specialists – accountants, engineers and technicians – in public-sector industry. They are workers too and a consideration of their problems is an essential part of a policy for public ownership.

The more serious misconceptions concern the need for a commitment of management to a socialist view of public ownership. Such a demand is impossible. Is it really suggested that all non-socialist managers and Board members should be dismissed and that a system of political appointees should be introduced? It needs no imagination to guess the trade union reaction. Would the Labour Movement tolerate a Conservative Government dismissing those who did not share their narrow conception of public ownership?

It is, of course, fundamental to the philosophy of public ownership that board members and senior management carry out the objectives laid down for the industries. One of the central themes of this book is that consistent guidelines for the industries have not been evident in the post-war years. It is unfair to hold the management of the industries entirely responsible for the failure to socialise public ownership when they have not been given a clear indication of what is expected of them.

6 Some Blind Alleys Explored

> My business habits had one other bright feature, which I called 'leaving a Margin'. For example; supposing Herbert's debts to be one hundred and sixty-four pounds four and two-pence, I would say, 'Leave a margin, and put them down at two hundred.' Or, supposing my own to be four times as much, I would leave a margin and put them down at seven hundred. I had the highest opinion of the wisdom of this same Margin, but I am bound to acknowledge that on looking back, I deem it to have been an expensive device. For we always ran into new debt immediately, to the full extent of the margin, and sometimes in the sense of freedom and solvency it imparted, got pretty far on into another margin.
>
> [Charles Dickens, *Great Expectations*]

Policies for the development of public ownership must cope with the dilemmas and conflicts discussed in the previous chapter. They present real problems and cannot be overcome by superficial formulas which fail to recognise the underlying difficulties. This chapter seeks to demonstrate this proposition by looking at three 'solutions' to the problems and identifying their shortcomings.

Saying 'the Government should let industry get on with it' places a degree of reliance on a free-enterprise system which no longer exists. It ignores some of the most powerful arguments for public ownership. On the other hand the interaction of supply and demand is important: the market does matter and there is no simple alternative which can be labelled 'socialist planning'. Workers' co-operatives may well become an important element in a socialist industrial policy but, at present, there are too many unanswered questions to suggest that workers' control is the answer to all Britain's industrial problems.

THE GOVERNMENT SHOULD LET INDUSTRY GET ON WITH IT

Two solutions are sometimes proposed by opponents of public ownership: the Government should avoid all state involvement in industry and should pursue an active policy of denationalisation; the Government should tolerate the existence of a public industrial sector but should not become involved in its operation. These two forms of the argument are closely connected. Both are based on the central assumption that the price mechanism and the market system, if allowed to operate unimpaired, are the best means of allocating resources.

Milton Friedman has become the most forceful advocate amongst those hostile to nationalisation in any form. In a provocative paper published in 1977 he argued that part of the shock treatment needed to cure Britain's economic problems was denationalisation, either by auctioning the industries or giving them away by establishing a mutual fund:

> These enterprises belong to the people; so we are going to give them to the people. This method has a big advantage. If you tried to auction these industries off individually, the Government would get the revenue and it would waste it. But if you gave it to the people and you allow a market to be established, you would see in a very short period that this would unsnarl itself. . . . You accomplish two purposes at once: you would reduce the Governmental deficit at the same time as you provide for a more efficient private economy.
>
> [Milton Friedman, *From Galbraith to Economic Freedom* (London: Institute of Economic Affairs, 1977) p. 52]

This is an extreme statement of the case. Most of those who are opposed to interventionist state industry recognise that some sort of public ownership is inevitable, and could be desirable. Their objection is to the introduction of non-commercial considerations in the operation of the industries:

> Our general conclusion, then, is that for the purposes of setting objectives for individual state undertakings and judging their efficiency, there should be a much stronger guarantee than exists now that these undertakings are in business rather than in politics. Most people do argue that state enterprises should be treated as being in business, but we have seen that undertakings which are nationalised cannot be in that position. There is need for a clear recognition of the desirability of competition among state enterprises, both among themselves and with privately-owned undertakings, as well as of the right of state enterprises to diversify. There should also be ready access to the open capital market, combined with a mixture of public with private ownership. Above all, indeed partly to expedite charges such as those just mentioned, the rights of ownership in public enterprise should be clearly defined. They should also be allocated to an organisation which is commercial in nature rather than to a Minister and his officials.
>
> [David Coombes, *State Enterprise: Business or Politics?* (London: Allen & Unwin, 1971) p. 237]

Many of the most persuasive arguments for public ownership are based on a recognition of the inadequacies of the price mechanism. The idea that nationalised industries should be entirely commercial in character is totally at odds with this justification for public industry. Supporting an entirely competitive public sector amounts, therefore, to a complete endorsement of the philosophy of the free market, though not necessarily of the capitalist system.

The study of the price and market mechanisms forms the basis of much of traditional economics. Since Adam Smith wrote *An Inquiry into the Nature and Causes of the Wealth of Nations* in 1776, economists have constructed theoretical models based on the uncluttered workings of the market system while the system has shown a continuing tendency to destroy itself. In theory the price mechanism operating to bring the supply and demand for all products into equilibrium results in higher rewards being given to those who are prepared to satisfy the greatest consumer wants. The producer, in intending to satisfy only his own gain, is led by Adam Smith's 'invisible hand' to behave in a way which promotes the needs of the whole society. Building on this foundation, and making a series of assumptions about how an individual achieves economic satisfaction, neo-classical economists were able to put forward the proposition that 'perfect competition' was the best form of economic organisation. The necessary conditions for the existence of perfect competition virtually defined the system out of existence: each buyer and seller should be small relative to the market; there should be perfect knowledge available to buyers; there should be easy movement between the different types of production.

One fundamental objection to perfect competition was the recognition of the existence of economies of scale. If larger production units could produce at a lower cost, the development of bigger firms should be tolerated. These firms could only be financed by capital which could come from internal or external sources. Internally the firm could build up finance for future investment in capital by making a profit; externally the firm could persuade investors to take a risk by lending their capital. Either way the 'invisible hand' operated. The customer continues to be king. By exercising his preference by spending his money on goods he values he leads to the best overall allocation of resources.

The growing concentration of industry and the domination of financial markets by institutions have, however, combined to reduce the ultimate power of the customer. The share of the 100 largest enterprises in manufacturing net output in the United Kingdom stood at only 16 per cent in 1909. By 1970 it had increased to 41 per cent. The rise of very big business is a worldwide phenomenon but it seems to have gone further in Britain than in any other comparable advanced economy. Equally the smaller manufacturing establishment, on the perfect competition model, has declined: in

1963 those manufacturing establishments employing under ten people provided only 2 per cent of British manufacturing output, compared with nearly 11 per cent in France and over 18 per cent in Italy [S. J. Prais, *The Evolution of Giant Firms in Britain* (London: Cambridge University Press, 1977)].

These dominant firms inevitably reduce consumer choice and, at the same time, raise the money for future investment mainly through retained profits – over half the investment finance is currently derived from this source. Borrowed money provides about half the remainder and the ordinary investor who provides 'risk capital' is declining in importance. The bulk of shares traded are, in any case, held by financial intermediaries. Between 1963 and 1973 individual shareholdings as a proportion of total shareholdings fell from 59 per cent to 42 per cent while the holdings by pension funds and insurance companies increased from 10 per cent to 28 per cent. The idea that the small investor can influence capital investment is a myth: studies have shown that less than 4 per cent of British adults directly own shares in British industry. The major institutional investors traditionally do not take a direct interest in the management of firms and the available information suggests that the capital represented by shareholders in attendance at company AGMs rarely exceeds 1 per cent of the total.

If investors do not actively seek to ensure that they achieve the maximum return on their capital, one of the necessary conditions of the free-enterprise system remains unsatisfied. An equally important condition concerns the role of the workers. They must be prepared to work for wages that are sufficient to maintain demand yet are not too great to prevent the firm remaining profitable. They must also accept closure and redundancy as a consequence of unprofitability. The refusal of workers to accept redundancy is a comparatively recent phenomenon but, as earlier chapters have shown, since the 1971 occupancy at Upper Clyde Shipbuilders it is no longer possible to design industrial policy which treats the workers as no more than another factor of production.

One of the most telling objections to the arguments of the 'free enterprise' school has been their failure to adapt their philosophy to these facts of modern industrial life. With conspicuous exceptions, they have remained committed to an idealised market system which scarcely, if ever, existed. Economic theory has, however, developed to take account of the changed industrial environment. Neo-classical economists explained business behaviour by inventing the 'entrepreneur', a single person who was both owner and manager; modern economists have recognised that the managers and the owners of modern corporations are distinct entities. Since the manager is in charge of operations, the firm is unlikely to pursue straightforward profit-maximising objectives. A number of 'managerial' theories of the firm have been developed to explain business behaviour in a way that is consistent with a recognition of this distinction.

The pioneering work in this subject was undertaken in 1932 by A. A. Berle and G. C. Means, who produced a book called *The Modern Corporation and Private Property* (New York: Harcourt, Brace and World, 1953). Berle and Means recognised that economic power was tending to concentrate, that the assets of large corporations were increasingly controlled by self-perpetuating managers, and that the capital market no longer exercised any effective constraints on the behaviour of management. They proceeded from these premises to argue that there was a tendency for managers to develop a social conscience which was quite different from the ethic of entrepreneurial capitalism. Forty years later the Confederation of British Industry attempted to validate Berle and Means by undertaking the discussions, already described, on the socially responsible company.

A number of different theories have been advanced since Berle and Means to describe the firm's behaviour. W. J. Baumol in 1959 suggested that management should try to maximise sales revenue subject to a profit constraint; R. M. Cyert and J. G. March in 1963 viewed the firm as a series of sub-organisations attending to different objectives in turn; O. E. Williamson in 1964 suggested that management try to maximise a 'utility function' whose principal components were the number of staff they control, the amount of fringe benefits and the company profits above a certain minimum level; R. Marris in 1964 suggested that management should try to maximise a combination of share valuation and company growth.

The best known managerial theory of the firm is the one outlined by the American economist J. K. Galbraith. Galbraith's arguments have developed over a series of books and now can be outlined in the following way. In a mature corporation power has passed to the technostructure –

the association of men of diverse technical knowledge, experience or other talent, which modern industrial technology and planning require. It extends from the leadership of the modern industrial enterprise down to just short of the labour force, and embraces a large number of people and a large variety of talent.

The aim of the technostructure is to make sufficient profit to ensure an independent life, to achieve maximum growth, and to produce things which are challenging to technological ingenuity. Since the technostructure dislikes uncertainty it moulds consumer tastes to suit its products and ensures that the Government provides the necessary conditions for the firm's survival. A planning system has replaced the market system.

This excursion into economic theory is necessary for the light that it throws on the statement under examination. Managerial theories of the firm suggest that 'the Government should let industry get on with it' can no longer be a plea for a throwback to a textbook market economy; the statement has to be recast as 'the Government should leave the allocation of resources to the judgement of the professional management who dominate industrial decision-making.' Two commentators would, however, disagree with this view of the industrial system. Both O. E. Williamson and Milton Friedman claim that modern industrial society still corresponds to the market system in important respects. The former, in a revision of his earlier views, has argued that large corporations have now reverted to a behaviour closer to profit maximisation since multidivisional firms with distinct operations will allocate resources to the most profitable division. Milton Friedman simply argues pragmatically:

Unless the behaviour of business men in some way or another approximated behaviour consistent with the maximisation of returns, it seems unlikely that they would remain in business for long. Let the apparent behaviour be anything at all – habitual reaction, random chance, or whatnot. Whenever this determinant happens to lead to behaviour consistent with rational and informed maximisation of returns the business will prosper and acquire resources with which to expand.

[Milton Friedman, *Essays in Positive Economics*
(Chicago: University of Chicago Press, 1953) p. 22]

It is, however, beyond question that the combined authority of modern management, corresponding to Galbraith's technostructure, gives them enormous power over the allocation of resources. This is true in both public and privately-owned industry, but ironically a recognition of this fact has resulted in the development of a major line of attack on public ownership alone:

In the free competitive market, the business man survived only if he satisfied the customer. By contrast, the bureaucrat or apparatchik in the command economy did not depend for his living, his security or his career prospects on meeting the public wishes. One system rewarded industry, flair, energy and imagination; the other orthodoxy, sycophancy and caution.

So proclaimed a nostalgic Sir Keith Joseph in 1976.

As 'enterprise' no longer exists, it is incumbent on its supporters to put forward proposals to restructure the current industrial system so that it corresponds to their ideal. Such practical proposals do not abound in the literature, though two were set out at the beginning of this section. The case for the market system is, however, separate from the case for the free-enterprise system as a whole. Even if the market is dominated by giant firms, both publicly and privately owned, should they not be encouraged to conform to market principles and let prices be set by the interaction of supply and demand? The growth of modern technology and the importance of the Government in supplying public goods have however cast doubts on this naive reliance on the market system as a means of allocating resources. A consideration of transport policy provides some examples of the difficulties.

On a purely theoretical level it is possible to demonstrate that free-market considerations do not necessarily give the right guidance to the Government. E. J. Mishan in *The Costs of Economic Growth* (London: Penguin Books, 1967) describes a community where everyone travels by public transport, taking an average of ten minutes. A number of people then buy cars and reduce their journey time to five minutes but this causes congestion and public transport times increase to twenty minutes. More people are then induced to buy cars until in the end all travelling times are longer than the original public transport time. Using economic terms, Mishan has demonstrated that individual optimisation does not necessarily lead to overall optimisation.

There are a number of practical objections to the market system which can also be illustrated by a consideration of transport policy. People are not always aware of their best interests, using this term without moral overtones. Car drivers rarely cost their own time and frequently underestimate the true costs of motoring. The distributional effects of the market system can also be undesirable: transport policy based entirely on private motoring would result in those sections of the community that cannot afford cars being placed in a very disadvantageous position.

The most fundamental objection to the market system stems, however, from the difficulties resulting from the long lead times between ordering and delivery in high-technology industry. In advanced economies only Government intervention can ensure that suppliers remain in business. The best example of this probably occurred in the market for electricity generating equipment. When the Central Electricity Generating Board found itself with too much capacity in 1977, one of the major suppliers was faced with the prospect of collapse. Government intervention was essential, not simply because of redundancy, but in order to guarantee the survival of the industry.

Government intervention in the market therefore seems to be inevitable. If this is accepted, the intervention should be institutionalised and the organisation of publicly-owned industry can help this to be successful. For this reason there seems to be little merit in the idea that nationalised industries should be encouraged to ape the behaviour of idealised 'free enterprise'. One other consideration follows from the previous discussion. Despite the existence of very real constraints, the technostructure does have an enormous amount of power. Managerial capitalism can mean that decisions on the allocation of industrial resources, the provision of employment, and the satisfaction of consumers are taken in an inappropriate framework. One argument for public ownership, therefore, should be that it provides the opportunity to design a more appropriate framework.

THE MARKET DOESN'T MATTER – WE NEED SOCIALIST PLANNING

This solution is the complete opposite of the previous one. Starting from a recognition of the inadequacies of free enterprise along the lines discussed, socialists have gone on to reject the market system and, in some cases, the price mechanism. 'From each according to his abilities, to each according to his need' is an explicit rejection of allowing the price of commodities to be set by the interaction of supply and demand. The extreme argument leads to support for a 'command' economy where goods are unpriced and are allocated by some sort of controlled rationing system. Convinced advocates of 'socialist planning' would not seek to dispense with the price mechanism altogether; they would, however, elevate economic planning into something approaching a complete solution to all our industrial problems.

Effective planning is essential in an advanced economy. However, as the economy becomes more sophisticated, so planning becomes more difficult. In this section some of these difficulties will be considered: the problem of effective forecasting will be outlined, the attempts to use planning as a panacea in the 1960s discussed and more recent developments examined. It is sometimes suggested that there are a number of economic techniques of planning and appraisal which are 'socialist'; these will be described in the final part of this section.

Planning is an attempt to shape the future towards predetermined goals. In practical terms it involves predicting the future pattern of the important economic variables, comparing this pattern with the one desired, and where discrepancies are identified, taking actions intended to alter the pattern. It has always seemed to socialists that this process is more likely to be successful where the planner has control of all economic resources. Hence the need for economic planning has always formed the basis of an argument for extending public ownership.

Certainly the fewer areas of uncertainty that are present, the easier it is to plan. For this reason it is less difficult to plan the supply of a commodity than its demand. The decision to produce is often vested in a comparatively small number of individuals, who have a great deal of control over production levels. The demand for a commodity is derived from a whole series of individual choices and, despite attempts to create demand by advertising and measure it by market research, a major dimension of uncertainty is introduced. This is true even where there are few customers for a product since their demand is derived ultimately from the final consumer; the Central Electricity Generating Board is the main purchaser of generating equipment in the United Kingdom but its requirements are dependent on the customer's use of electricity.

All planning depends on accurate forecasting and how difficult this can be is well illustrated by the problems that the Electricity Council and the Central Electricity Generating Board have experienced in forecasting electricity demand since the 1950s. Despite the expertise available, the satisfactory prediction of the rise in consumer requirements has proved too difficult and, as a result, changes in the Generating Board's ordering pattern for new equipment have caused a severe crisis amongst their suppliers.

The size of the electricity generating system that is needed is determined by the peak demand for electricity – simultaneous maximum demand. The statutory obligation on the electricity industry to provide a service to its consumers and the long lead times for power station construction make a smooth ordering policy extremely difficult to achieve. In 1972 the Chairman of the Board, Arthur Hawkins, told the Select Committee on Science and Technology that the growth in electrical load was expected to be between $3\frac{1}{2}$ per cent and 5 per cent a year. In the event growth was much lower: demand for electricity was actually 3 per cent lower in 1975/6 than in the previous year and based on demand forecasts no new power station orders would be placed before 1979 or 1980.

The Electricity Council's forecasting methods have been strongly criticised, especially by the Open University's energy research group. However, the research group's conclusion – 'It is misleading and dangerous to try to use historical trends to predict future demand. Ultimately the growth in demand for electricity depends on the growth in ownership (and application) of electrical appliances' – shows just how difficult a problem the Council faces. As the sophistication of planning trends have increased, so technology has made forecasting more complex and made the idea of a centrally planned economy more difficult.

In 1964 planning was the centrepiece of Labour's election manifesto: 'Here is the case for planning and the details of how a Labour Cabinet will formulate the national economic plan with both sides of industry operating in partnership with the Government.' The much heralded National Plan was published in November 1965. It was based on the predictions of individual industries about future rates of growth; details on overseas trade and the international economy were fed in. The result was a valuable analysis of the problems to be overcome in achieving a growth in the national product of 25 per cent between 1964 and 1970, designed to persuade industry to invest with confidence. Unfortunately the Plan was stillborn. In July 1966 the Government announced a pay freeze and no one could plan for expansion. Instead of the 4 per cent annual rate of growth called for by the Plan, the annual rate of growth was nearer $1\frac{1}{2}$ per cent. The National Plan never became a self-fulfilling prophecy; and never progressed beyond wishful thinking.

One fundamental problem of planning should be of great concern to socialists, but they have begun to face up to its consequences only recently. Planning places considerable power in the hands of a small number of people. It is no answer to say that the modern industrial state, having departed from the traditional model, itself places power in the hands of the small group of people who constitute the technostructure. Milton Friedman's expression of the problem should make all socialists feel uncomfortable:

> If the free market is not the ruler, who are the rulers? Not according to Galbraith, entrepreneurs serving the market, but technocrats, who have no moral authority. Besides, they are not disinterested. These technocrats are self-selected, they make their own jobs, they appoint one another. What right do they have to decide people's tastes, or how the resources of the community should be used? If you had Adam Smith entrepreneurs running society in response to the demands of the public, that would have some moral authority. But the technocrats have no moral authority: they are running it in their own interest.
>
> [*From Galbraith to Economic Freedom*, pp. 32–3]

One of the strongest arguments for industrial democracy is that it can lead to a dispersion of power within the planning system. Unfortunately, the specialists have traditionally had a monopoly of knowledge and expertise. The long-standing Labour Party distrust of the Civil Service is derived from sentiments similar to the ones expressed by Friedman. For this reason alone, the dangers of establishing an industrial policy based on centralised planning should not be underestimated.

Another series of problems derive from practical difficulties in the planning process. In a modern society there has been an enormous increase in the amount of decisions that need to be made if the economy is to be controlled. To make these decisions information is needed and this is not always available at the time it is required. The amount of uncertainty has increased. Further, this information cannot always be obtained by the planners without difficulty. Consider the problems surrounding the introduction of planning agreements heralded in the 1975 Industry Act.

The fact that the first planning agreement took around fifteen months to complete reflects the apathy, and at times hostility, shown towards the idea by private industry. The fact that the first such agreement was made with Chrysler (UK) Ltd illustrates another truism: companies which are likely to require Government support for their activities are much more likely to be open and forthcoming than those that can manage without it. This need not be seen as a problem relating exclusively to private ownership; industrial chauvinism has been all too evident in nationalised industries. If those with privileged access to information decide to be deliberately obstructive the responses available to the Government are very limited. Planning agreements are much more likely to be successful as moves towards industrial democracy progress.

Despite the inherent difficulties outlined in this section, planning is vital. The lags between ordering and delivery that are characteristic of advanced technology makes the consequences of underestimating the pattern of future demands very costly. Planning is therefore an important aspect of economic management, whatever form of economic system is operated. It is sometimes claimed, however, that there is an approach to planning which is characteristically socialist and which is innately superior to the more orthodox methods.

'Socialist Planning' can be used to imply one of three different things: orthodox planning which is undertaken by socialists; planning in an economic system where the resources are owned by the state; planning using socialist tools of economic appraisal. The first two definitions fail to recognise that many of the difficulties inherent in planning are caused by technical complexity. Because the planner happens to have one set of political sympathies, or his work is monitored by a committee including representatives of the trade union movement, it does not necessarily mean it will be more successful. Similarly, the experience of estimating electricity demand shows that planning inside the framework of nationalised industries does not eliminate the problem.

Does socialist planning occur then, when planners use socialist tools? There has been growing interest in recent years in an attempt to develop a means of economic assessment which looks at a wider range of an organisation's activities than the ones which appear on a balance sheet and a profit and loss account. Cost-benefit analysis has attracted particular attention. This technique can prove very useful in focusing attention on several dimensions of a problem, but it should not be oversold.

Cost-benefit analysis proceeds by attempting to place money values on those aspects of a project which are not priced – these are known as externalities. The practical difficulties are considerable. The Roskill Commission on the Third London Airport, which sat for two and a half years, cost over £1 million and had its recommendations overturned by the Minister, faced the problem of estimating the costs of aircraft noise. It attempted to solve it by comparing the value of houses in noisy and quiet areas and removal costs, ignoring the fact that many people would not move whatever the circumstances. Considerable criticism, and a lively correspondence in *The Times,* ensued when the Commission considered valuing a Norman church at the sum for which it was insured against fire. The standard 'COBA' method used by the Department of the Environment for road appraisal includes an element which costs the value of time for a number of categories of individual: the time of a mother with two children on a bus is calculated at less than a fifth of the value of the time of a salesman in a car. One commentator has described cost-benefit analysis as 'nonsense on stilts' and an attempt to convert genuine political and social issues into bogus technical ones. [Peter Self, 'Nonsense on Stilts: Cost-Benefit Analysis and the Roskill Commission', *Political Quarterly* Vol. 41, No. 3 (1970) pp. 249–60]

This judgement is harsh. Cost-benefit analysis is an emergent technique, but because of its arbitrary nature it is open to abuse. This does not detract from the case for a wider examination of business activities and in this context the reports of the journal *Social Audit* deserve consideration. A social audit is described as an independent, systematic monitoring of corporate social performance and the journal contains a number of practical examples of the art. The last report to be published, 'On the Avon Rubber Company Ltd' (spring 1976), is the most interesting. The report describes the way in which the company 'has interpreted and discharged its responsibilities to its employees and consumers, to the people who live with it, and to the physical environment in which they live – and indeed, to anyone who might be affected by what the company has done'. The Avon Rubber Company co-operated but disagreed with the conclusions.

The company was audited under a number of headings: pay and fringe benefits, job security, participation, health and safety, race relations, consumer products and services, advertising, air and river pollution, waste disposal, energy use, external noise, community involvement and others. Social Audit itself did not present an overall balance sheet involving judgements as to whether some social cost may be justified in the light of another benefit. The technique is exploratory and as yet imprecise – but it still adds up to an important development.

Perhaps the most exciting recent initiative which involved a wide examination of a company's activities came not from an external body, but from a shop stewards' committee. In 1974 the Lucas Aerospace Combine Shop Stewards' Committee held a meeting with Tony Benn, then Minister for Industry, who told them of the likelihood of cutbacks in employment in aerospace. He advised them to consider alternative uses for company resources.

Their response was to produce a detailed report suggesting diversification into a number of new engineering fields including components for low-energy housing, fuel cell technology, and braking systems. The company's formal response, however, was lukewarm. Although the shop stewards' plan stressed the need for corporate social responsibility and emphasised employee rights, it did not depend on methods of economic appraisal which were uniquely 'socialist' to give it relevance. Its merit lay in the fact that it represented an aware and concerned internal response to the problems of change.

WORKERS' CONTROL IS THE ANSWER

One alternative to orthodox industrial policy has gained wide support on the left in recent years: it is argued that large industrial organisations operating under workers' control should be the predominant form of organisation and that they should be supported by a system of socialist planning. These two strands of the new policy are potentially contradictory. 'Socialist planning', as previously discussed, can be an argument – albeit an ill-defined one – for a highly centralised form of control. Workers' control, by giving the ultimate power to the producers, is the most decentralised form of industrial organisation. The contradiction, at its simplest, can be illustrated by a consideration of the consequences of a clash of objectives between the workers in control and the requirements of the planning system.

Whether 'workers' control is the answer', therefore, depends on what is expected from the industrial system. This in turn depends on whose point of view is being considered. The most important distinction, of course, lies between the impact that workers' control can have in enhancing the interests of the workers themselves and the impact that it can have on the interests of the consumer and the community as a whole. A recognition of this distinction lies at the heart of the most powerful argument against workers' control.

As has already been mentioned, Sidney and Beatrice Webb were amongst the strongest opponents of the syndicalist movement dur-

ing the important wave of widespread interest which occurred at
the beginning of the twentieth century. The Webbs were strong
supporters of state socialism where the ultimate control of the
economy would rest with a representative body chosen by the voters.
In a major book, written deliberately to offset the influence of
syndicalism, the Webbs identified

> cleavages of interest and purpose between the producer of a
> particular service or commodity and the consumer, and also
> between producer and consumer and the interests of the whole
> body of citizens, many of whom neither produce nor consume
> the particular product, including notably the interests of future
> generations.

These cleavages are highlighted by the Webbs as the major objection to workers' control. The conflict of interest between producer
and consumer is the most obvious: 'The very concentration of the
members' attention, not on the market place, where the demands
of the consumers are paramount, but on their own particular work-
shop is inimical to success'. [Sidney and Beatrice Webb, *A Constitution for the Socialist Commonwealth of Great Britain* (London:
London School of Economics, 1920) p. 156] The conflict between
producers and society as a whole can occur when the workers mis-
use the resources allocated for production:

> The self-governing workshop, or the self-governing industry,
> necessarily producing for exchange, is perpetually tempted to
> make a profit on cost: that is to say, to retain for its own mem-
> bers whatever surplus value in the price for which it can dispose
> of its product. . . . Further, in the practical administration of its
> own industry, a Democracy of Producers, whether it be of manual
> workers or of brain workers is, by the very nature of its member-
> ship perpetually tempted to seek to maintain existing processes
> unchanged, to discourage innovations that would introduce new
> kinds of labour, and to develop vested interests against other
> sections of the community of workers.   [p. 156]

Nearly sixty years later these sentiments were echoed in the National
Consumer Council's evidence to the Bullock Committee on Industrial Democracy. Their submission drew heavily on the work of the
Webbs: 'The carve-up between capital and labour that the TUC's
proposals could produce could only too easily be at the expense of
consumers whose prime interest is in the efficiency of industry.'

The significant omission [of consumer concern in the TUC docu-
ment] highlights the great weakness of the aspirations for work-

ers' control embodied in syndicalism: the employees of a particular company or industry, if left to themselves, are almost bound to arrange things so that it suits them, which is by no means necessarily the same thing as suiting the wider community.

[National Consumer Council, *Industrial Democracy and Consumer Democracy: Seven Reasons Why the TUC is Wrong* (London, 1977) p. 2]

Where the Webbs made a particularly strong case is in disposing of the argument that workers' control is synonymous with democracy. The Webbs illustrate their point by a consideration of the position of trade unions and local authorities. The union executive and the local council have the responsibility of carrying out the policy required by members and electorate; it would be inconsistent with that view of democracy to allow policy to be determined by the full-time union staff or the council officials. If they had had the advantage of post-war experience the Webbs would have certainly added the example of the health service: no one in the Labour Movement would argue that the hospitals should be run for the benefit of the doctors.

A recognition of these clashes of interests clearly calls the philosophy of workers' control into question. Unfortunately this argument can be taken too far. The strident tone adopted by the National Consumer Council against the TUC proposals was particularly unfair. It is one thing to argue that the TUC proposals for parity representation are not likely to produce anything of positive benefit to the consumer; it is quite another to argue that they would necessarily work to his detriment. The discussion in a previous section showed that the current structure of industrial organisation was geared to serving managerial values rather than the interests of the consumer. There is no reason why altering the pattern of managerial authority in the way that the TUC propose would hurt the consumer interest.

One further objection to workers' control is centred round the problems of managerial accountability. Can a system of workers' control fulfil the tasks currently undertaken by management? This question is not straightforward. Before attempting to answer it is necessary to distinguish between the tasks undertaken by management and the status that management needs to carry them out. Four broad management functions can be listed: identifying problems, making decisions and plans, implementing the decisions and plans, providing the information for all of this to be done. These functions could still be performed under a system of self-management, though in a somewhat different way. What is altered, however, is the system of accountability for decisions.

Orthodox management theory holds the individual manager

responsible, within the hierarchy, for undertaking these activities. He is then held accountable for the results of his actions. Patterns proposed for workers' control vary, but under the most popular system, a controlling council of workers would appoint managers who would then undertake to implement the council's decision. Can management in this system have the status they need to preserve a form of accountability? At present there is insufficient practical experience of the operation of workers' control to answer this question, and the small-scale co-operatives in existence cannot, by themselves, be regarded as providing the necessary evidence. It is unfortunate that professional management have – because of their instinctive hostility to industrial democracy in anything but the most mild form – failed to address themselves to this problem.

One other set of difficulties surrounding the introduction of workers' control deserves some consideration. There is little evidence of widespread support for self-management within the rank and file of the trade union movement. The previous chapter showed how the new worker co-operatives were born more out of a reaction to redundancy than genuine commitment to the co-operative cause. Further, their survival was heavily dependent on the determination of strong leadership. Some degree of commitment to the principle of self-management is a precondition of success and its absence in practice undermines the suggestion that it can form the basis of an industrial policy. This statement must be qualified, however, as there has been no positive attempt by the Government to promote the idea.

All these objections relate to the design of an entire industrial system based on workers' control. The case for encouraging self-managing units to operate, along the lines of the new producer co-operatives, within the framework of a more mixed system, is quite separate. The problem of the 'cleavages of interest' need not arise if the unit, by operating in the way that the workers wish it to operate, fulfils a function which is needed by society as a whole. The Meriden motor-cycle co-operative, producing for a highly competitive market, is scarcely in a position to exploit its consumer.

Finally, it is worth considering whether a system of workers' control is in the best interests of the workers themselves. The answer is not as obviously 'yes' as might appear at first sight. There is an underlying danger of stressing industrial democracy at the expense of internal democracy and underestimating the importance of the trade union as a separate channel of representing the workers' interests. A recognition of this danger has led to the opposition amongst some trade unions to the Bullock proposals. Amongst socialists it is recognised that whatever form of worker participation in management is favoured, it must be accomplished through the trade union movement. It is, therefore, unclear how a conflict between the interests of the workers and the interests of the enterprise would be resolved under a system of self-management.

In any case there is a strong possibility from the workers' point of view of self-management not leading to the sort of traumatic changes that are expected. In practice, Yugoslavian experience has suggested that, despite the establishment of worker co-operatives, a great deal of power still resides in the hands of management – see, for example, T. Adizes, *Industrial Democracy: Yugoslav Style* (New York: Free Press, 1971) and J. Obradovic, 'Workers Participation: Who Participates', *Industrial Relations* xiv (1975) pp. 32–44. The provision of information underlies all the other management functions and those with a monopoly of technical expertise are in a powerful position when it comes to deciding what to present and how to present it. 'Decisions' that should be taken at management meetings can be pre-empted by a judicious choice of information which rules out all but the favoured alternative. So far there has been a dearth of empirical information on this important problem.

All the above arguments are presented to suggest that, at present, workers' control cannot be offered as a complete solution to all the problems of public ownership. They in no way, however, detract from the need for progress towards industrial democracy in some form. Industrial democracy can be a vital element in reducing conflict, but there is a danger in overselling it as a political principle. Equally, nothing that has been said suggests that worker co-operatives could not become an important strand in the development of a socialist industrial policy. What is needed, however, is a realistic assessment of their potential and a positive programme for their development.

7 Can Common Ownership Meet the Challenge?

> This island is too small, its economic life too precariously balanced, its geographical situation too vulnerable, for its fate to be left to the casual workings of chance or the insatiable unheeding drive of the profit-makers. Jarrow is an object lesson in what happens then. The profiteers having ravaged a town or a country can take themselves and their gains elsewhere. The workers have the main stake in their homeland, for in it they must remain.
>
> [Ellen Wilkinson, *The Town that was Murdered*]

The argument advanced so far is that there are significant areas of conflict underlying effective industrial policy, and that there are no panaceas which will enable them to be overcome without difficulty. This fact may appear obvious – yet it has rarely been explicitly recognised in political dialogues on industrial policy. Once it has been accepted, the role of public ownership can be considered from a different standpoint. Supporters of nationalisation must demonstrate how a transfer of ownership can help to cope with this conflict. The proposition developed in the remainder of this book is that the elimination of private ownership, while not in itself offering a complete answer to all industrial problems, is necessary to give the Government the tools with which to achieve its policy objectives.

This proposition will be illustrated by a consideration of the arguments that are used to support public ownership against private ownership; arguments which have inevitably been altered by the changing structure of private ownership. Public ownership is needed for a variety of different purposes and this suggests that a variety of different responses will be required. Post-war experience shows that there has been a failure to develop these diverse forms of organisational response and that, in order to cope with the indus-trial problems that are likely to be encountered in future, the Labour Movement should rediscover its commitment to common ownership – not just nationalisation through the vehicle of public corporations.

The orthodox case for public ownership is that it is needed to give the Government power. Tony Benn, replying to the debate at the 1973 Labour Party Conference, argued:

> Our policy on public ownership is based upon a serious analysis of the developing power structure in our society: fewer larger companies, many of them multi-national, growing larger and

more powerful, and we know, and we must say that if we do not
control or own them, they will control and own us, and that is
the challenge that we face. It is not just a matter of efficiency,
it is not just a matter of regional policy. It is a matter of political
power. . . .

[LPACR (Blackpool), 1973, p. 185]

Although this statement of the case for public ownership would
command wide support in the Labour Movement, it stands in need
of two important qualifications. First, power does not exist in isolation, it must be related to the goal or objective which is to
be achieved. In industrial policy the Government will need different
methods to achieve different goals; until these are specified it is
impossible to say how powerful a weapon public ownership can be
in any individual case. Secondly, although ownership can give
power, power itself is not simply a function of ownership. This
qualification was well illustrated in the consideration of private
ownership contained in the previous chapter. Although nominal
power is vested in the shareholder, effective control lies in the hands
of professional management, who operate under a number of important constraints. There is a great danger, when designing a
policy for public ownership, of reacting to a form of free enterprise
system that no longer exists.

The role of public ownership must, therefore, be considered
against the background of modern industrial society, and in the
context of the Government's objectives in that society. The aim of
the industrial system as a whole has already been discussed. It exists
to take inputs, process them and produce an output that the customer values more than the sum of the inputs. This surplus of output over inputs must be produced efficiently without exploiting the
workers; it must also be distributed in an acceptable way. The
modern industrial system, with its mixed pattern of ownership, to
some extent performs this function, but socialists have identified a
whole series of deficiencies both in the results that it achieves and
the way that they are achieved. A recognition of these deficiencies
provides a useful starting-point for the design of a new industrial
system. Before considering them in detail, however, one general
point about the present system needs to be made.

It would be surprising if the separation of ownership and control
in private industry did not dramatically affect the case for public
ownership. In fact, it has reduced the relevance of one traditional
argument, but created a more powerful new one. The effective
elimination of the entrepreneur means that both power within the
corporation and the wealth generated from its operations are less
likely to be accumulated in a few hands. Effective power is dispersed over Galbraith's 'technostructure'; the problem of the un-

even distribution of wealth is now recognised to be one which goes far beyond the question of industrial ownership.

Even if private ownership had no impact on wealth distribution, the structure and behaviour of the private firm would still be a matter of concern to socialists. The divorce of ownership from control has given rise to a new stronger justification for Government intervention. In the current system of shareholder ownership and managerial power, decisions on the allocation of industrial resources, the provision of employment, and the satisfaction of consumers are being taken in an inappropriate framework.

The legitimate interests of stake-holders in the performance of an industrial organisation have already been identified. Effective industrial organisation must find a way of achieving the objective of the enterprise, whilst effecting a fair compromise between these potentially conflicting interests. The argument that the modern industrial corporation can do this is of diminishing acceptability. The consumer suffers as his choice is diminished by growing industrial concentration; the worker is regarded as just another factor of production. The underlying conflict between management and owner has been hidden by shareholder inaction. The frequent local reaction to factory closure has focused attention on the absence of a mechanism to resolve the opposing interests of the corporation and the community.

Far from enhancing the industrial system, the mechanism for private ownership has at best a neutral and, on occasions, a negative impact. Since shareholders rarely, if ever, exercise their power, one potential dimension for the control of the industrial corporation is removed. This imbalance leads to a variety of shortcomings in industrial policy and can give a number of useful indications for the design of effective public ownership. Nationalisation has developed, in the main, as a response to the failings of private ownership and a number of distinct policy objectives for public ownership can be specified directly from the deficiencies of the modern corporation.

The most widely accepted role for public ownership is as the supplier of essential commodities. This role includes some of the major public corporations and is an area where the case for nationalisation commands acceptance across the political spectrum. The case gained early acceptance in respect of the public utilities, particularly gas and electricity. It has historically been recognised that these commodities were in a different category from those usually traded on the market, for two reasons. They were essential rather than luxury goods and a basic requirement if an individual was to have an acceptable standard of living. Secondly, they were natural monopolies: they could only be supplied efficiently if one supplier was allowed to take advantage of the economics of scale. Since a private monopoly would, unless the Government were prepared to exercise meticulous control, be capable of making extortionate profits, the Government should take on the responsibility of supplier.

At the heart of this argument is a recognition that the market system cannot supply all the goods that the community values. Once this argument is accepted in respect of public utilities, it can be extended to justify state ownership in a number of other areas. Private ownership has on occasions failed in a number of key industries whose performance is vital to the rest of industry. Where the inefficiencies of these industries, or their threatened collapse, has a detrimental effect on the rest of the economy, there is a clear case for public ownership. This was the justification for the nationalisation of steel and of the machine tool firm, Alfred Herbert Ltd, whose shares were vested in the National Enterprise Board in 1975. The nationalisation of Rolls-Royce in 1971 illustrates a new variant of the case for public ownership as a supplier of essential commodities. Although the RB211 engine could not be described as an essential good, the survival of Rolls-Royce assumed an urgency which went far beyond defence and international obligations.

When a country is involved in the production of goods which are extensively traded internationally, the risk of complete corporate collapse is unacceptable. This is particularly true in high-technology industries. Government action may be needed, not only to counteract spectacular collapses like Rolls-Royce, but also to alleviate the gradual decline that the UK shipbuilding industry has experienced and which seems likely to continue. If home-based industries are experiencing difficulties, they must be supported to ensure that the nation maintains a presence in the international market. Extinction would not only result in heavy localised unemployment but also destroy one area of potential exports. This argument can be expressed in another way. There is a need for a wide national industrial base to guarantee long-term economic survival. Since this must include a number of high-technology exporting industries, the Government must intervene to ensure their continuation, and public ownership is an essential weapon for this.

If this deficiency in the market system has been recognised historically, so equally has a second deficiency. An earlier reference has been made to the way that the price mechanism can fail to take account of 'externalities', the costs and benefits for which no charge is made. These need not always be trivial, sometimes they can be so fundamental that any decisions based solely on figures which enter the profit and loss account would be incorrect. Transport generally provides the best example of this category: the way the argument is usually expressed is that transport should be run for service rather than profit.

The market system is recognised to be inoperable where the price

mechanism cannot function. It is inappropriate to argue that the
commuter in London should be provided with the transport system
that he is willing to pay for, when fares are set by administrative
fiat. The only way that the commuter can express his preference for
better services at higher fares is by voting for a candidate whose
views happen to coincide with his every four years in an election
for the Greater London Council. Since the determination of the
desired level of service cannot be made by the market system, different considerations must apply. Here an additional point should be
made: it is generally recognised that a low level of service in transport has a particular impact on low-income groups. Equity considerations are therefore relevant and these fall outside the scope
of the market system.

Public ownership may therefore be needed to make good the
deficiencies of modern capitalism when it fails to provide essential
goods or when allocation by the price mechanism is inappropriate.
Three other shortcomings of the market system provide arguments
for the development of public ownership. First, that the imbalance
between public and private wealth can only be corrected by the
use of profitable public enterprise. Secondly, that public enterprise
is needed to counteract the influence of multinational corporations.
Thirdly, that a Government response through public ownership is
needed to correct regional employment imbalances.

The growing resistance to taxation which has been identified by
Chancellors of the Exchequer from both parties poses a particular
problem for socialists. One way of ensuring that greater resources
are available to the Government would be to allow nationalised
industries to run up a surplus. This argument achieved a great deal
of prominence in the early 1970s when the Conservative Government began to hive off the profitable ancillaries of the existing
public corporations. Supporters of public ownership, and in particular the Public Enterprise Group, were able to argue that the profits accruing to the public sector reduced Government dependence
on taxation and national insurance. The 'revenue' argument was
also used to support the establishment of the British National Oil
Corporation in 1975. If the economic recovery based on offshore
oil is to lead to growth in public sector facilities, as well as private
consumption, a Government stake in the industry is essential.

The earlier discussion on the pricing policy of the existing public
corporations demonstrated how it was designed to keep trading
surpluses to a minimum. The profitable corporations have tended,
therefore, to be those which are less likely to be directly in the
public eye, the British Airports Authority for example, or the subsidiary companies of the large industries. In these cases surpluses
are less likely to be a source of political embarrassment. Addition-
ally, it has always been recognised that the scope for revenue-raising

corporations is limited to those areas where there is no opportunity for monopoly suppliers to exploit captive consumers.

The need for the Government to extend public ownership as a counter to the multinational corporations has arisen almost entirely in the post-war industrial environment. A well-publicised illustration of the conflict between the policy of a multinational corporation and the national interest was provided in 1971 when Henry Ford, in the course of a serious strike, threatened to withdraw car production from the UK in the event of sustained labour difficulties. The size of the Ford investment in the UK was so great that it was almost impossible for them to pull out completely, but the transfer of even part of the capacity elsewhere could have had serious repercussions on local employment and supplying industries.

One possible Government response would have been to take over production after the Ford company had withdrawn; another would have been to intervene to prevent foreign-owned companies dominating key sectors of the economy. The Italian State Holding Companies have been used by the Government for both these purposes. In the UK the Industrial Reorganisation Corporation performed a similar function between 1966 and 1970: for example in 1968 it intervened to organise a merger between Britain's three ball-bearing manufacturers and prevent control of the industry passing into Swedish hands.

The other major role for public ownership which results from the shortcomings of the market system has already been identified in earlier chapters. It has been recognised, since the days of Keynes, that there is no guarantee that the economy will operate at full employment. Fiscal management may be able to affect the level of overall demand, but, even ignoring the argument of how successful it may be at the national level, there are likely to be gross regional inequalities in employment opportunities. Public ownership has been advocated as a way of compensating for the imprecision of fiscal policy.

Nationalised industries have been used as a tool of Government regional policy on a number of occasions, but the role has been mainly negative, for example the slowing down of the rate of colliery closures. The positive role of public ownership as an instrument of job creation has only begun to attract attention in recent years. Once again the comparative success of Italian public sector industry has influenced the Labour Party. The first important new response came, in 1975, with the creation of the Scottish and Welsh Development Agencies.

This list of the potential roles for public ownership in modern society is not meant to be exhaustive. Each of the categories described has, however, already resulted in the creation or increased activity of some form of publicly-owned industrial organisation. As industrial society changes so the argument for public ownership is likely to change in emphasis. In addition, some extensions of public ownership will be justified by definite and unique arguments, rather than as a method of achieving a broader policy aim. The best historic example was the Government's nationalisation of licensed premises in Carlisle and parts of Scotland in 1915 and 1916 to control the consumption of alcohol amongst key munition workers. A further example of state industry that could be set up for a specific purpose is the derelict land reclamation agency proposed in the report of the Hunt Committee. [White Paper, *The Intermediate Areas*, Cmnd 3998 (London: HMSO, 1969] Although such an agency would have an impact on regional employment policies, the case for its establishment rests almost entirely on environmental grounds.

The problem facing the Government is to design a structure for public ownership with these purposes in mind. The objectives which these purposes imply are quite distinct and potentially contradictory. It is impossible, for example, to design an enterprise with the objective of raising the maximum amount of Government revenue while at the same time providing the best possible level of service. It should also be recognised that although public ownership is a key characteristic in each of the categories considered, it is very much the lowest common denominator rather than the highest common factor. The elimination of private ownership is a necessary condition for each of the categories, but in all other respects the form of organisation likely to be required for the successful fulfilment of their objectives is very different.

Social changes will produce new roles for public ownership and new problems which require the elimination of private ownership of industry for their solution will arise. There will therefore be a need for continuous experimentation with new forms of industrial organisation to meet these new demands. It is against this background of change that the socialisation of industry, the positive gain to consumer, worker and the community, must take place. The idea that an experimental approach to industrial organisation is required fits somewhat uneasily with orthodox socialist thinking, which always seeks for a total solution. However, Clement Attlee hinted at it in 1937:

All the major industries will be owned and controlled by the community, but there may well exist for a long time many smaller enterprises which are left to be carried on individually. It is not possible to lay down a hard and fast line on the constitution and management of every industry. There will no doubt be wide diversity in accordance with the requirements of particular undertakings.

This diversity does not necessarily develop as a matter of course. Attlee went on to define a set of essential conditions for successful public ownership:

> The first of these is that the interest of the community as a whole must come before that of any sectional group. The second is that managers and technicians must be given reasonable freedom if they are to work efficiently, a freedom within the general economic plan; while the third is that the workers must be citizens in the industry and not wage slaves. The exact way this will work out will again depend on the circumstances of the particular industries. In the organisation of industry there are to be considered the interests of the community as a whole, the interests of producers, and the interests of consumers. Each interest has its particular sphere in which it must be paramount.
>
> [Clement Attlee, *The Labour Party in Perspective*
> (London: Victor Gollancz, 1937) p. 153]

The idea that there should be 'wide diversity in accordance with the requirements of particular undertakings' is an important one. Effective organisational design is impossible unless the purpose of the enterprise is defined. The starting-point should be an unambiguous, internally consistent statement of an organisational purpose, from which a set of objectives can be derived. This argument may appear obvious, but in practice it is frequently forgotten.

Consider the case of the major organisational initiative introduced by the 1974 Labour Government, the establishment of Britain's first State holding company, the National Enterprise Board. The euphoria with which the Labour Party embraced the Italian system of public ownership has already been described. At the time there was a powerful case for the establishment of a State holding company but it was unreasonable to suggest that it alone could be the 'financial and managerial base for promoting new public enterprise'. Unless the role of the NEB is altered as a result of internal or external pressure, or unless its staff show remarkable managerial skills, it will disappoint. It cannot achieve the high expectations and contrary demands made on it.

According to the 1975 Industry Act, the purposes of the National Enterprise Board are the development or assistance of the economy, the promotion of industrial efficiency and international competitiveness, and the provision, maintenance or safeguarding of productive employment in any part of the United Kingdom. The Board's functions are described as assisting the development of any undertaking, promoting or assisting in reorganisation, and extending public ownership into profitable areas of manufacturing industry. In addition the Board is charged with the promotion of industrial democracy and holding and managing securities.

With such an indeterminate set of objectives it will be virtually impossible for the NEB to achieve results which would be recognised to be successful. The criteria for success that have been set are inadequate. The gap between the reality of what the NEB can achieve and the performance expected from it is enormous and will inevitably be a future cause of controversy. What makes this particularly depressing is that, even with the limited resources available to it, the NEB has already proved itself more than capable of fulfilling an important role in the economy.

In its early operations the NEB's investment has been dominated by its holding of Rolls-Royce and British Leyland shares which together amount to almost 85 per cent of its portfolio. The existence of these major holdings does not result from deliberate decisions by the NEB in support of its purposes. They have been acquired by the Government and vested with the Board. The positive interventions that the Board has made in the field of computer peripherals, machine tools, office systems and electronics could well prove extremely valuable in the future. However, the role that the Board can play is curtailed by financial limitations – the NEB has a borrowing limit of £700 million – and the ability of its staff of fifty to cope with the demands made on them. Opponents of public ownership will criticise the NEB for doing too much; supporters of public ownership will be reticent in defending it as its performance will disappoint them. Judged against the high expectations aroused at the 1972 Labour Party Conference its achievements will not be great. Judged against the background of its financial base its achievements will be substantial.

For the NEB to operate successfully, and to be seen to do so, a number of changes are necessary. There must be a realistic recognition of what can be achieved by this form of organisation; objectives must be set which make these achievements possible; it must be given adequate funding and staffing. Most important, a State holding company should be seen as one element amongst the many that need to be employed, not as a method of complete salvation. There is not one single failing of private ownership that can be corrected by public ownership; the defects are many and various. Different problems need different solutions. Successful control is impossible unless a sufficient range of responses is available to match the requirements of the situation. This is a first principle of general control theory. The Government is attempting to regulate a very complex industrial system so it will need to be able to command a wide range of possible organisational responses.

Judged by this criterion, the attempts that have been made to design the structure for public ownership since the war have been deficient and unimaginative. The universal reliance on the basic public corporation structure, scarcely altered since 1933, has been described in Chapter 2. The 1961 and 1967 White Papers were the only important attempts to clarify the initial statutory objectives and it was not clear from these documents why the industries were in public ownership at all. Each of these attempts to design public sector organisation, the public corporation and the White Papers, was meant to apply to every nationalised industry. This blanket approach disregards the very different purposes that relate to the different organisations. Such attempts to differentiate between corporations that have been made were undertaken on a timid, almost *ad hoc* basis: public dividend capital, for example, seems to have been introduced in a particularly arbitrary manner. No wider social objectives have been introduced for any of the transport industries. This shortcoming should be of particular importance to socialists who have traditionally argued that nationalisation provides an opportunity for moving beyond narrow criteria for industrial control. Until the drive for greater industrial democracy began to achieve its first successes, and this has already been identified as stemming from the trade union movement not from the Government, there have been few initiatives in the control of nationalised industries which could be described as socialist in any sense.

The developments in the design of public ownership that have taken place have been characterised by a general desire to muddle through somehow or other, and a permanent switchback between centralised and decentralised organisational forms. The electricity industry provides an illuminating illustration. In 1954–5 a Committee under Sir Edwin Herbert was established to examine the industry, which at the time in England and Wales consisted of a Central Electricity Authority overlording a number of Area Boards. The Herbert Committee identified failures due to too many headquarters conferences, and to insufficient discretion being allowed to Area Boards. The Committee proposed to effect improvement by separating the executive and supervisory functions of the Central Electricity Authority and they recommended that executive responsibility should be transferred to a new Central Electricity Generating Board. With some amendments the Minister accepted these recommendations. In 1958 the CEGB was established together with a new Electricity Council which took on many of the old Electricity Authority's responsibilities.

In 1974 another committee under Lord Plowden was established to cover the same ground. In its report, published in 1976, its main recommendation was the following:

After considering the weaknesses of the present structure and reviewing possible structures in the light of the guiding principles which we have discussed, we recommend the unification of the industry. A single statutory body should take over the functions of the Electricity Council, CEGB and Area Boards. For the rest of this report we shall refer to this body by a name revived from the industry's past – the Central Electricity Board (CEB).

[White Paper, *The Structure of the Electricity Supply Industry in England and Wales,* Cmnd 6388 (London: HMSO, 1976) p. 24]

What, one may ask, will the 1994 Committee of Inquiry recommend?

Changes in the organisation and the operating rules of publicly-owned industry should be seen as an inevitable consequence of a developing society – not as a once-every-twenty-years choice between centralisation and decentralisation. The Government must develop this flexible approach to industrial problems and it is appropriate to review the responses that are available. It is here that the Labour Movement's commitment to common ownership – already defined as public ownership together with other types of non-private ownership including co-operative and municipal ownership – should be recalled. The range of Government response to the problems of the industrial system is broadened if the full complement of the forms of common ownership is included. Some of these forms, like the public corporation and consumer co-operatives, are well known and well-developed; others, like municipal trading, are of less importance currently. There are attractions and limitations in each form.

Public corporations have already been discussed fully and a large number of criticisms of them set out, but there is much more potential in this method of public ownership than the previous comments might suggest. The overwhelming need is to make public corporations a more flexible form of response. They are likely to continue to be the standard pattern when the Government wishes to ensure the continued supply of essential goods or capture external social costs and benefits. However, the differences between public corporations should outweigh their similarities. Their main advantage relative to the other forms of common ownership is the close co-ordination with Government industrial policy that can be achieved by the determined use of public corporations. Unfortunately this has been absent in the past and the corporations have been given a high degree of autonomy. Government directives have rarely been used.

The changes that will result from the introduction of industrial democracy in the corporations should be regarded as an occasion for experiments in their development. The effective representation of stake-holder interests and the introduction of non-commercial objectives are the two most important areas for experiment. It cannot be emphasised too strongly that the design of these corporations should be related to their purposes.

Public ownership in the form of state shareholding was an impor-

tant element in industrial policy long before the National Enterprise Board was established. The range of shareholdings has been
wide and many have been acquired for unique historical reasons –
the UK Government shareholding in the Suez Canal Company,
which was taken up in 1876, provides an interesting case in point.
Generally, when the Government has extended public ownership in
the form of shareholding it has emphasised that its interest will be
kept at 'arm's length' on the pattern of a normal shareholder. Beagle
Aircraft Ltd is an outstanding example.

Beagle Aircraft Ltd was founded in 1960 to develop and manufacture light aircraft. In 1968, two years after the company had
experienced difficulties which needed extensive Government support, the Minister of Technology acquired all the assets of the company and established a wholly government-owned company. In 1970
the Public Accounts Committee of the House of Commons investigated the arrangements and expressed concern on the inadequacy of
information available to the Government. The Government replied
that:

> When the Government creates or acquires such a wholly Govern-
> ment-owned company to carry on a commercial undertaking, it
> expects the Board and officers of the company and those doing
> business with it to proceed on a normal commercial basis with
> full regard for the legal rights and duties of the various parties.
> The Treasury and the Department of Trade and Industry agree
> that arrangements between the Government as a sole shareholder
> and a wholly-owned commercial company must be such as to en-
> able Government to be adequately informed of the company's
> policy and progress, but with due regard for the need to give the
> Board the proper degree of freedom to manage the affairs of the
> company commercially and without prejudice to the legal rights
> and responsibilities of the Board and its officers and of those
> doing business with the company.

[From a Treasury minute set out in Merlyn Rees, *The Public Sector
in the Mixed Economy* (London: Batsford, 1973) p. 219]

State shareholdings, held on this basis, may be the appropriate response when public ownership is required to obtain an economic
surplus or as a response to multinational corporations. The development of a State holding company has given an added dimension to
this form of intervention, but earlier discussion has shown how the
NEB in its present form is likely to be a singularly blunt instrument. The Government's use of shareholdings need not imply support of the system of private ownership, merely that an arm's-length
arrangement is preferred. This obviously has its disadvantages as
well as its advantages.

A wide range of options is provided by co-operation. Co-operative principles have traditionally had an attraction for the Labour Movement which has not been extended into legislative support. In 1973 the Labour Party proclaimed that:

> Public ownership does not mean a rigid adherence to the 1940s form of nationalisation. The best example of our wider view is the Co-operative Movement, where eleven million people join together to operate a huge sector in the British economy, which has a vast potential for further development.
>
> [*Labour's Programme for Britain 1973* (The Labour Party, 1973) p. 35]

The best known co-operative activities in the United Kingdom are, of course, the consumer co-operatives which operate in the retail market. They are owned by their customer-members and after a period in comparative decline have re-emerged as a forceful trading organisation. During the 1950s the Retail Co-operatives had consistently maintained about 11 per cent of total trade, but in the following decade they underwent a decline which reached a trough at about 7 per cent. The period was characterised by cut-price competition and aggressive marketing from the rival multiple stores. The situation was reversed and the market share recaptured in the mid-70s.

Part of the co-operative response has been to attempt to procure mergers between the locally controlled and independent societies. There were 704 societies in existence in 1965 compared with 540 just three years later. By 1977 there were only 215 societies in existence. However, unquestionably the price of this rationalisation has been a loss of commitment from the members. Voting at elections for the Board of the London Co-op, for example, is an activity in which less than 1 per cent of the members participate. The Co-operative Movement is of course well aware of its own problems.

The extension of co-operative principles in industrial organisation is attractive, but the scope for Government support is necessarily limited by the voluntary basis of the idea of co-operation. It could be difficult for Government support to be acceptable without diluting the principle of self-help. One area where this need not apply, and that has been successfully developed in Scandinavia, is the support of the Co-operative Movement to keep retail options open to the consumer – by subsidising uneconomic rural shops for example.

For some time the Labour Party has been committed to the idea of a Co-operative Development Agency. The idea emerged initially towards the end of the 1960s, and was mentioned in the 1970 and October 1974 manifestos. Since the idea has not proceeded beyond the drawing-board, the purpose and form of organisation of the Agency remains imprecise. Inevitably the interest in the new producer co-operatives in the mid-70s, a form of common ownership which has been fully discussed in earlier chapters, has resulted in some change in emphasis. At various times potential roles for the Agency have included the following: aiding the mergers of retail societies; encouraging modernisation in societies by providing capital; stimulating and financing research into methods of improving efficiency; improving management and staff training; helping 'co-operative democratic structures in housing, farming, and other ventures'. Such an Agency would obviously have an important part to play in developing co-operation as a form of response.

One final form of organisation should be considered, though it has been far less developed than the others that have been considered so far – the option of municipal ownership. Local authority-based enterprises have become more limited as gas, electricity and, most recently, water supply have been taken away from municipal hands. Most of the current activities relate to market trading, catering or abattoirs, though certain near-anachronisms remain. Kingston-on-Hull for example runs a telephone exchange and Birmingham a bank. These unusual municipal activities arise through historic accidents reinforced by unique legislation. General development of municipal activities could only be encouraged by general legislation.

Local authority-based enterprise is, of course, a very decentralised form of response. Although most forms of municipal trading would be expected to be profitable, there is also an argument for developing more comprehensive forms of local response to employment problems, for example employment co-operatives. This form of activity could challenge the tight control of local authority expenditure that the Government has exercised in recent years. Nevertheless, the movement amongst some Councils to safeguard local employment in this way is most welcome and could make an exciting contribution to wider Government policy if the right support was offered.

Before concluding this chapter it is desirable to present a brief summary of the argument advanced so far. A number of logically distinct roles for common ownership in our society have been identified, all of which stem from a recognition of various inadequacies of the current industrial system. Common ownership, however, should be seen as more than a repair mechanism for modern society and its positive advantages should be recognised. The forms of response based on common ownership that are available to the Government have also been discussed.

There must be a conscious attempt to develop these various forms of common ownership. They must be made more flexible and must be adapted to meet the new challenges made on the Government in an evolving society. In the next chapter the ways in which this could be achieved will be considered. Before proceeding to this analysis, however, it is necessary to provide answers to several fundamental political questions asked in the field of industrial organisation. These questions can be expressed in three closely interrelated ways: 'Is ownership relevant? Is there any future for private ownership? Should the Labour Party continue nominally to support a mixed economy?' Each will be considered in turn.

Ownership is relevant. The arguments advanced in this chapter have thrown a new emphasis on the case for common ownership as a method of controlling the industrial system. Common ownership gives society the power to design an appropriate industrial system. The nominal ownership of industry by shareholders is, as has been said, not merely neutral, it removes an important dimension of restraint on industrial activities. The case for public ownership, compared to other forms of common ownership, is that this dimension can be reintroduced. The Government is able to use its power of ownership to ensure that broader interests are taken into account when decisions are made within the industries.

There is little that can be said positively in favour of the existing system of private ownership. The system does, it is true, ensure that some of the nation's resources are saved and invested rather than spent, but it does so by a tortuous and outdated method. Investment is financed in two distinct ways: by higher prices for the goods purchased, which can then become retained profits; by saving through pensions funds and insurance societies. The first of these methods is, for the individual, a form of involuntary savings and is inconsistent with the widespread acceptance of the need for a policy of price control. The second method is becoming more and more haphazard as the link between individual savings and the support of profitable industrial activities has disappeared. The boom in property prices of the early 1970s was the most disturbing manifestation of this phenomenon. Pension funds and insurance societies were outbidding each other in forcing up the prices of empty office blocks at a time when investment in industry was collapsing. Moreover, within the rules of the game, they were doing the right thing by their investors.

The collapse of private industrial investment, the elimination of shareholder involvement, the growing power of the 'technostructure', the increasing domination of key markets by a handful of producers, are all symptoms of a system in decline. The most powerful argument against 'managerial capitalism' is that its supporters do not seem to be unduly perturbed about the state of the system they advocate. Except for the brief discussions about the social responsibilities of the company they have made no overt recognition of the problems of private ownership – except, that is, for the frequent attacks on Government 'interference'. These attacks are characterised by a nostalgic throw-back to a system that no longer exists. The complacent tone of the private sector opposition to the form of industrial democracy advocated in the Bullock Report was totally at variance with the state of their system. It is for those who see some merit in shareholder ownership of industry to put forward reforms for the system. While the private sector is so deficient, the public sector will continue to be used to remedy the inadequacies of the private sector quite irrespective of the political arguments.

What then, of the mixed economy? The argument developed throughout this book has been an argument in favour of a mixed industrial system in the sense that the Government needs a mixed response to industrial problems. This does not imply, however, support for an assertion that the boundaries of public ownership should not be allowed to extend beyond a certain limited proportion of industry as a whole. The aim should be to develop the whole variety of responses of common ownership; the part that public ownership will play will be determined by the type of industrial problem faced by the Government and the success in developing other responses. Some pattern of private ownership will be needed in the foreseeable future for smaller businesses and services, but while shareholder ownership remains such a sterile form of organisation its future remains in doubt.

8 Towards Socialised Industry

> With socialists it is not a question of 'socialising', at one blow or in any way, the whole of industry, and all services, but of providing the most advantageous form of administration for each industry or service, as, one after another, each passes from capitalistic to public ownership and control.
>
> [Sidney and Beatrice Webb: *A Constitution for the Socialist Commonwealth of Great Britain*]

Effective industrial policy can only be achieved if a variety of forms of common ownership are developed. This will require the introduction of new organisational structures and operational rules; the 'primary purpose' of the commonly-owned industries will vary and different patterns will be required for different purposes. A blanket approach is no longer appropriate. The socialisation of industry must therefore be undertaken against a background of change. Changes are needed if public-sector industry is to meet the challenges posed by an advanced society and this must be seen as an opportunity to give positive benefits to consumers, workers and the community.

This chapter will consider how a system based on common ownership can be used both to meet the requirements of Government industrial policy, and at the same time to move towards socialised industry. The role of Government, industry and employee will be considered in turn and a number of conditions necessary for the system to work will be discussed. What is proposed is not another 'panacea' which, if introduced immediately, could solve all the problems of the industrial system overnight, but a number of guidelines which together could enable the right form of organisational response to evolve.

Before turning to a consideration of the ways of designing the different structures and developing appropriate operational rules, one important qualification needs to be made. Public ownership cannot eliminate all the conflict in an industrial system. The discussions and case studies presented have sought to demonstrate how conflict will inevitably result from the different demands of the various stake-holders; nationalisation does not, in itself, cause them to wither away. The most obvious illustration of continuing conflict under public ownership has been the one between efficiency and redundancy.

Because effective common ownership is essential for the future of the industrial system, a method for coping with this conflict must be developed. This problem should be tackled in a number of ways. First, the stake-holders themselves must be explicitly involved in the design of the organisation and in the establishment and monitoring of objectives. This means that the traditional role of management will be transformed, a subject that will be discussed at fuller length, and that, in an important sense, the 'arm's-length' relationship between Government and the industries will be altered. Secondly, if conflict is to be structured the relative strengths of some of the stake-holder groups will need to be increased. Thirdly, as was argued in the earlier discussion of industrial democracy, where there is conflict it must be resolved within a bargaining framework. The formal recognition of the different interests of worker, consumer, and the broader community will help to resolve conflict only if there is a trade-off between the various groups.

A further condition for this system to work successfully is that information must be freely available to all parties. This provides the most powerful argument for the creation of worker-directors. The defensive atmosphere of secrecy which characterises British industry has already been observed, and the issue has become confused by the failure to recognise the distinction between private information and corporate information. The need for personal privacy is a subject which lies well outside the scope of this book. Corporate information is needed if rational economic choices are to be made. Morrison expressed this point well:

> Within proper limits it may be necessary for us to concede that the public interest requires privacy in a certain restricted field, particularly, in the transition period, when capitalist interests which have so far survived may desire to make trouble. But the principle which socialised industry should aim at applying is that the nation, which is the proprietor of the undertaking, has the right to the maximum possible knowledge about the undertaking. For economic science – a very different thing under socialism from much of the twisted stuff served up under that name to capitalist society – in order to render the fullest public service, must be well equipped with the actual facts of industrial production.
>
> [*Socialisation and Transport*, p. 229]

The problems in designing these new forms of common ownership can be considered at three interrelated levels: Government, industry and employee. 'How may the effectiveness with which the Government uses common ownership to fulfil the aims of its industrial policy be increased?' is a first-level question. Second-level problems relate to the ways in which the effectiveness of the industries in achieving their objectives can be improved; it is at this level also that the main impact of socialisation will be felt. The third-level problems are the most widely known: 'How can the part that the workers play in industry be enhanced?' has now become a fashionable question.

The Government's role is easy to define in principle but full of difficulties in practice. It should specify the various purposes for the individual enterprises and they will be derived from its overall industrial aims. It should then design the structure of the enterprises to ensure that these purposes will be fulfilled without undue strain on the organisation. However, as organisations become more and more complex they cannot be controlled from the centre and some sort of decentralised control is needed. This poses a very real problem. What guarantee is there that decisions taken in a decentralised organisation are always consistent with advancement towards the overall aim?

This problem is present in all situations of industrial control. How, for example, can a multinational corporation ensure that its subsidiaries achieve their objectives? The standard answer to this question is by setting profit targets, but these have no validity unless adequate resources are available to the subsidiary for them to be achieved. It would be counter-productive to deny the subsidiary the resources and then try to run everything from headquarters.

Stafford Beer, a cybernetician who was closely involved in the restructuring of Allende's Chile, expressed this problem generally:

Every manager, whether he runs the family business or a small department in a firm, whether he runs the firm itself or a major department of Government, whether he runs the country or an aspect of international affairs, faces an identical problem. He faces, that is, the need to maintain a viable system far more complicated than he personally can understand. And the beginning of wisdom for management at any level is the realisation that viable systems are, in large measure, self-regulating and even self-organising. . . . The sensible course for the manager is not to try to change the system's internal behaviour, which typically results in mammoth oscillation, but to change its structure – so that its natural systematic behaviour becomes different. All of this says that management is not so much part of the system managed as the system's own designer. What are the aspects of the system with which management can sensibly interfere, which it can design or redesign? They are the mechanisms of that system: the structures, and the rules governing the behaviour of structures, which are usually taken as given.

[Stafford Beer, *Platform for Change*
(London: Wiley, 1975) pp. 105–6]

To socialists concerned with the development of effective public ownership this is a new and perhaps alien concept, but the alternative of total control from the centre is unworkable. This alternative was discussed in the course of the examination of blind alleys in Chapter 6. The weapons that the Government can use for organisational design include striking the appropriate balance between stake-holders, the provision of an appropriate form of finance, and the agreement of objectives. Unfortunately, since there have been only limited experiments with different forms of public sector organisation, there is little practical experience available on how these weapons can be used to produce the desired effect.

A practical illustration could be helpful at this stage. Supposing the Government wishes to establish a new public corporation to bring employment to a depressed region; what considerations should be used in its design? The Government, in providing finance, fulfils its function as a stake-holder, but it should be accepted that the interests of the community, expressed through the medium of local authorities, should be a key factor in decision-making. Local authorities should therefore be represented on the boards. Further, there is no point in agreeing an organisational objective which is not correlated closely with job creation. If the wrong set of objectives is set, the introduction of capital-intensive rather than labour-intensive industry to the region could be regarded as successful, although it had failed to achieve what it was designed to do.

The Government's main job, then, is the design of the whole system of common ownership, and it should be held accountable for its success or failure. For this reason, there is no case to be made for interposing an institution between the Government and the industries. Accountability is already blurred in the case of Rolls-Royce and British Leyland, which report to the Department of Industry through the National Enterprise Board. Some commentators have advocated the establishment of an intermediate holding company between the Minister and the industries to insulate them from Government 'interference'. This argument rests on an assumption about the undesirability of Government involvement which is totally at variance with the views advanced in this book.

As well as designing the system the Government is responsible for providing an acceptable economic background in which it can work. What form this will take will depend on the system that is envisaged, but one point is likely to be true almost irrespective of the detailed options chosen. Public ownership is unlikely to be effective unless the Government pursues much more vigorous measures to reduce unemployment and to counteract its worst economic effects. This is a truism whatever sort of economic system is advocated, but the underlying point needs to be developed to illustrate an important aspect of a policy for public ownership.

Public ownership does not eliminate unemployment. Shifts in demand and improvements in technology will inevitably lead to the rundown of both factories and industries. While the difference in status and economic power between being in and out of work remains so wide, it is scarcely surprising that even the most traditionally moderate workers are showing increasing resistance to redundancy. Overmanning is not a real economic problem if alternative employment is unavailable. If it is available, however, there is a danger of atrophy in the industrial system. The only way of breaking into this vicious circle is to take a more positive attitude, first by reducing the effects of unemployment and secondly by increasing the retraining facilities available. In Sweden, for example, 2·4 per cent of the workforce undergo training annually compared with 0·25 per cent in Britain.

How can the industries achieve the objectives laid down for them without exploiting the stake-holder groups? This can be best achieved by ensuring that stake-holder interests are explicitly recognised and can influence the decision-making process, though this need not necessarily take the form of direct representation on the boards of the industries. In the course of the discussion on industrial democracy in Chapter 3 it was seen that worker-directors could only be one aspect of the movement towards giving workers a greater say in the running of the industries. The alternative way of achieving this result that was presented, the extension of bargaining, may be appropriate as far as the interests of some of the other stake-holders are concerned.

The groups who have a legitimate right to a say in the industries have already been identified as workers, managers, Government, consumers, and, on occasions, local government and major suppliers. The importance of each particular interest will vary from industry to industry and so will the way in which their view can be made effective. The role of the workers and consumers has already been discussed and some further aspects will be considered later in this chapter. In this new design proposed for socialised industry the role of management will be significantly altered: they must be seen as workers who have a central role in the system of accountability that needs to be established. The Government, in their capacity as the providers of capital, represent the interests of the community at large in so far as they must ensure that resources are not misused.

The explicit recognition of the role of local government is not the novel suggestion that it appears to be. As economies of scale dictate the emergence of fewer, larger production units the impact that large employers will have on the local communities will increase. The closure of Rolls-Royce would have had a devastating effect on Derby, as the closure of steelworks will have on Cardiff and Ebbw Vale. While the nationalised industries have never denied the rights of the local authorities, a more explicit recognition would be positively helpful.

Socialised industries will be designed by the Government in a way that reflects the need to satisfy the primary purpose; this will be achieved by an organisation which reflects the right balance between the stake-holders, by a relevant form of financial structure, and by specifying appropriate objectives. The first job to be undertaken at the industry level is to translate these objectives into meaningful and mutually acceptable means of regulating the industry's performance.

The direct involvement of the stake-holders in this operation is essential if the semantic problem, the gulf between those inside and outside the industry, is to be overcome. Stafford Beer expressed this difficulty succinctly:

> What is difficult, and what makes the whole question so fraught with electoral danger is the attempt to specify a mode of control in a language which makes sociological sense to the electorate and operational sense to the managers in charge of the industry simultaneously.
>
> [*Decision and Control* (London: Wiley, 1966) p. 376]

This difficulty will only be avoided if all the interested parties have a say in the formulation of the targets.

This problem of semantics has contributed to some of the alienation between the nationalised industries and the community. The most common expression of this alienation is for outside commentators to attack the public corporation management as bumbling bureaucrats; one example was cited in Chapter 5 where the attack on steel industry management made by a Tribune MP at the 1975 Labour Party Conference was reproduced. Equally, senior steel industry management have, on occasions, made their distaste of politicians all too clear. This manifestation is singularly unfortunate and had its roots mainly in the clash of personalities and in the uncertain policies for the industry. As serious, however, are the frequent local authority attacks on nationalised industries that are made at public inquiries and in other stages during the planning process. This sometimes has a tragi-comic aspect: nationalised industries are accused simultaneously of total incompetence and of undertaking a deeply-laid conspiracy against the community. This contradiction is simply a reflection of the underlying alienation.

Once the objectives have been translated into acceptable targets progress towards them must be monitored. It is here that the role of management must be recognised. Managers must accept the responsibility for the achievement of the targets and for recommending the changes necessary to overcome problems. This cannot be done unless they are involved in the formulation of targets and are given adequate resources to make their attainment possible. Socialised industry cannot therefore be successful unless the role of management is recognised to be a legitimate one. A necessary condition for the successful monitoring of targets is that the information is available.

One further point should be made about operations at the industry level. External efficiency audits may, under exceptional circumstances, be of use, just as the National Board for Prices and Incomes produced some helpful reports in the late 1960s, but the value of a general audit agency is dubious. The possibilities of outside experts coming in and diagnosing fundamental problems which have escaped the notice of concerned people within the organisation is more remote than it is fashionable to suppose. It is far better to use internal or external expertise to work in co-operation and at the behest of the enterprise, since the power of management to withhold co-operation from unwelcome intruders is considerable. The involvement of stake-holders in the establishment and monitoring of targets is an important step towards exposing internal problems. In any case, all too often the solution proposed by management consultants takes one of two forms: greater centralisation or greater decentralisation. Sometimes these can be offered in successive inquiries into the same organisation.

In general there is far too much deference shown towards anyone who claims 'expertise' or acts as a 'consultant'. This stems in part from a lack of self-confidence on the part of the ordinary worker and manager in industry and is totally at variance with the values of the Labour Movement. One particular problem should be recognised: the 'consultants' and 'experts' generally have a background and experience which must divorce them from shop-floor problems. This would not matter if Britain was not such a class-ridden society. Since it is, there is an inevitable danger of all the expertise appearing to work against the interests of the workers. This, incidentally, is also a problem inherent in any organisation concerned with central planning.

The main third-level problem has already been set out: 'How can the part that the workers play in the industry be enhanced?' Less than five years ago the question would not be how this could be achieved, but whether it should. The growing support for industrial democracy evinced by people who have been in a position to do something positive towards it, but in practice have done nothing, should rightly be viewed with suspicion. There is however a real recognition that work should be made more satisfying and meaningful, and also that the current state of technology is working in the opposite direction.

Most of the management writers who are frequently quoted are

concerned with research that relates purely to the problems resulting from orthodox considerations. An exception is the study of the
motivation to work published by Frederik Herzberg in 1959. He
made a distinction between 'hygiene' factors in work and 'motivating' factors. Research demonstrated that when people were unhappy
it was the hygiene factors that caused it, amongst which were poor
supervision, inadequate salary, and inadequate working conditions.
When people were happy it was associated with the motivating
factors, for example a sense of achievement, recognition, satisfying
work, or responsibility. This research suggests that positive satisfaction at work will not be attained unless the individual is given
more scope and opportunities for self-respect.

This conclusion will come as no great surprise to socialists whose
political antecedents have argued for a different role for workers
since the industrial revolution began. Management research has
merely caught up with their fundamental belief of the dignity of
the individual.

Moreover, it is important to recognise that there are several
different ways in which the dignity of the individual can be enhanced. This comes back to a point made in an earlier chapter of
this book: the argument on workers' rights has been dominated by
discussions on industrial democracy to the detriment of a consideration of other dimensions of the problem. A share in decision-making
is a prerequisite of socialised industry, but so also are ways of making work more satisfying and breaking down the class structure
within industry.

The problems involved in shared decision-making are the problems of industrial democracy. These were fully discussed in an
earlier chapter. Alternative ways of achieving shared decision-
making must be seen as such; they are not ends in themselves. The
only general comment required at this stage is to underline that no
method will be successful unless it recognises the potential conflict
of interests between the workers and the other parties. Industrial
democracy must be rooted in the bargaining framework and based
on the trade unions. This places a considerable responsibility on
trade unions for ensuring their procedures are sensitive to grass-
roots feelings.

Once an industrial structure has been agreed, how can work be
made more satisfying within that framework? This topic has attracted increasing interest in recent years and there is now some practical evidence available from foreign, mainly Scandinavian, experience. Many of the issues are summarised in Lisl Klein's *New Forms
of Work Organisation* (London: Cambridge University Press, 1976).

One aspect of the growing interest in work organisation concerns
the experiments in job restructuring away from assembly lines.
Instead of the individual worker undertaking a simple repetitive

and monotonous job he is given the opportunity of contributing to the end-product in a more satisfying way, often as part of a team. This is a reaction against the sort of job fragmentation associated historically with Frederick Taylor, 'the father of scientific management', at the turn of the century.

Major scope for the application of these principles lies in the motor industry and the most important attempts have taken place in Sweden. At the Volvo plant at Kalmar, the assembly line has been replaced by individual carriers, each loaded with a car body travelling round a large circle. At various points the carrier can be shunted on to sidings for specialist operations, but most of the time it keeps moving. Teams are assigned to individual cars for related operations designed to give them the feeling that they have done a complete job. Individuals who want to see the body through all its stages can ride along with the carrier; the team also has some control over the speed of the carrier. This might not seem an over-radical innovation, but the fact remains that few workers who have experienced even this degree of control over their working life would wish to return to straight assembly line methods.

The financial balance of such innovations is uncertain. Generally the cost of building a plant for the new work systems is higher; Volvo's Kalmar plant cost 10 per cent more than a conventional plant designed to produce a similar output. Running and training costs may be higher and the planning of supporting services may be more difficult. On the other hand, labour turnover and absenteeism will be significantly reduced. There is insufficient evidence available to come to a conclusion on where the balance, in narrow financial terms, lies.

It is fair to say that in the British trade unions there has not been a great deal of interest to date in the potential of new forms of work organisation. In part this reflects an alienation from a system in which labour has historically been treated as just another factor of production. One argument which is sometimes advanced should be completely disregarded: there is not a shred of evidence that assembly line workers prefer boring and repetitive work. This argument is particularly elitist and distasteful when it is advanced by commentators who have never done this sort of work themselves. The fact is that most workers have never been given the option of any say in work design and, as they have no expectations, are unlikely to ask for it.

One other way of enhancing the dignity of labour should be discussed. There is an overwhelming case for dismantling the barriers that divide categories of workers into different status groups and for the elimination of discrimination based on sex, race or religion. Despite a better record of progress than the private sector, few women have attained senior positions in the public corporations.

In 1977 four industries included one woman as a board member: the British Airports Authority, British Airways, the National Enterprise Board and the National Bus Company. There were fourteen women amongst the 123 members of the various national and regional boards in the electricity industry. There were no women members at all on any of the other major boards. Although no published information is available this pattern is almost certainly repeated amongst senior appointments below board level.

The record of the nationalised industries in abolishing status differences also compares well with the private sector, but far too many petty differences still remain. Different status is also reflected in different entitlements to pensions, sick leave and holidays which are not so petty. There is no justification for these distinctions apart from a general belief in the merits of a class system.

There is one corollary to this argument that cannot be avoided. Is there any case for different levels of pay? Socialists would like to be able to answer no, and the Meriden co-operative described earlier shows equality can be achieved, but most recognise that the harsh facts of the domestic and international market for skilled labour dictate otherwise. This is only part of the answer, however. Active advocacy of the cause of greater equality of earnings will create the climate in which moves to greater equality become possible. It is for those who support it to be more positive in their arguments and also, if they are in a position within industry to do it, to lead by example. Until then the best that can be hoped for is that the rate for the job will apply and that status differentials will be abolished.

To summarise the argument so far: the socialisation of industry must be tackled at the interrelated levels that have been discussed. Changes will be needed in Government policy, in the operation of the industries themselves, and in the role of the workers. For socialised industry to function effectively, however, a number of necessary conditions must be satisfied. Three are of particular importance. A clear commitment to efficiency within the industrial system is needed; the power of some stake-holder groups must be strengthened; a new philosophy of management must be developed.

The political importance of efficiency in public sector industry has already been discussed. Nothing causes so much opposition to the Labour Party's economic strategy as the idea that nationalised industries are inefficient. Chapter 2 showed how much of the general criticism was misconceived, and how many of the public demands were inconsistent – no price increases but financial surpluses required, for example. In part it seems that nationalised industries simply have to bear this criticism. They are easily identified; a failure by them is blamed on nationalisation, a failure by private industry on British workmanship. Passengers on internal flights which have been run by privately-owned companies have been overheard blaming delays on nationalisation.

Socialisation must involve a positive gain to the consumer and the community. It is therefore important that the Government, in the first instance, seeks a clear commitment that common ownership enterprises use the resources at their disposal efficiently; and that it does so itself in the case of public ownership. The resources used must not be squandered; apart from any other consideration, there is a clear obligation to future generations. This does not mean that industrial policy should be harsh on the individual. It is an evident waste of economic resources to make workers unemployed when there is a need for what they can produce.

Once again the important thing is that objective facts are available. When falling demand or technological change mean that the production from a group of workers is no longer needed, the Government must take on the responsibility as part of its broader employment policy. If jobs are not available, the Government can have the option of intervening to ensure a more gradual rundown of labour and thus avoid hardship. In part, of course, this is done in the nationalised industries today. There is a further danger in not having a clear policy for employment: local communities will understandably use whatever pressure they can to oppose the run-down of local industry. The growing tendency to lay on professional public relations campaigns is disturbing. Objectivity will be sacrificed if the loudest voice always wins.

A further condition for the successful operation of socialised industry is the strengthening of the relative power of some stake-holder groups. The Government, management, and, where appropriate, the local authorities are able to take care of themselves. At first glance the same would appear to be true of the workers, but one qualification needs to be made. The importance of good communications between the shop floor and their representatives who are involved in decision-making cannot be overstated; this is one reason why it is essential that the trade union movement is used as the channel for industrial democracy. Better internal democracy within the unions then becomes even more urgent.

The other major stake-holder group, the consumers, will need to develop a much more effective voice. The Government must consciously seek to create a consumer constituency to represent the interests of all customers other than the major industrial purchasers. The diffuse distribution of consumers makes this a difficult but not impossible task.

Local centres can serve as the channel for grass-roots complaints and suggestions which can then be forwarded to the consumer councils. These new strengthened councils can be housed together with shared facilities and provided with sufficient expertise to give them the opportunity to become an effective counterweight. The industry councils could be part of the National Consumer Council and would provide the consumer representatives for the decision-making process in the industry. Their other functions would include the development of codes of practice and advertising for the industries. There is a clear danger of such a solution becoming very bureaucratic and remote from the ordinary consumer. There is also the danger of consumer councils experiencing the same drawbacks as an external efficiency auditor, which were described earlier. There is no easy answer to this problem, but its solution is obviously of vital importance to the success of socialised industry.

The third necessary condition for the successful operation of socialised industry concerns the acceptance by management of their role in the structure. This will depend greatly on a change in attitudes and the emergence of a new ethos. The function of management has already been described: managers are central to the whole system by acting as the agents of accountability. They must accept this role while undertaking the traditional management tasks of problem identification, decision-making and planning, and implementing the decisions. They must recognise that decision-making should be widely spread and they must be particularly conscious of the need to provide the information required for this to be successful.

Management can, therefore, no longer jealously guard its power and status. Unquestionably the adoption of the system of socialised industry advocated will result in a loss of management power compared with the existing system. This will inevitably lead to considerable resistance to changes. What is essential, therefore, is the development within management of a group who recognise the need for change and are prepared to argue the case for constraints on their power. The job of management in socialised industry will, if anything, be rather more exacting and challenging than at present.

There are distinct signs of a recognition amongst managers that they are workers too. As industry becomes more concentrated, and the manager-owner entrepreneurs disappear, so the old public-school-tie view of management is ending. The growing organisation of managers into trade unions is a welcome sign, as is the growing affiliation of management trade unions to the TUC – most significant was the recent affiliation of the British Association of Colliery Management. It is not a long step from a realistic acceptance of their new status to a realistic discussion of their new role.

Some aspects of the traditional ethos should remain. Objectivity in the presentation of the information for decisions is part of the good manager's rule-book; it will become even more important under the new system. The need for fair and realistic information is a theme that has emerged again and again throughout this book.

The alternative to objectivity is partiality and managers must be particularly wary of assuming that their values are the values of the organisation. This is especially important when considering selection and promotion decisions.

Conservative spokesmen on industry have never understood how offensive nepotism is to the manager who has earned his promotion the hard way. Equally, socialists have never recognised the degree of support that they could gain by opposing it. Nepotism is often felt to be excusable if the Chairman's son or son-in-law has 'spent his first year or so on the shop floor as an ordinary worker to get the feel of the industry'. This should be recognised for what it is: 'starting at the top and working your way up'.

Meritocracy, determining position by merit, is certainly preferable to nepotism. There is, however, a danger of a self-perpetuating system with managers reinforcing their own values by selecting aspirants who share them. One of the pioneering works on the theory of the firm, that by Berle and Means in 1932, argued that the separation of ownership and control had led to a desirable tendency of managers to develop a corporate conscience. If this were true, it would not be without its attendant problems. The growing sponsorship of the arts and sports by business organisations represents the decisions taken by management on the allocation of resources which do not belong to them. There is evidence that the chosen areas of sponsorship tend to echo management tastes, not those of the community at large: show-jumping not greyhound racing is given support.

The development of a new management style can be assisted by positive Government support. It would be desirable, for example, to encourage much more movement between public-sector industries. This would have the advantage of breaking down the 'industrial chauvinism', the excessive loyalty towards their own industry, that some managers have exhibited, which is probably seen at its worst in the energy industries and has been evident in some public corporation annual reports. It would also have another favourable effect. The pattern of public-sector management, in terms of the consideration given to individuals, has so far closely resembled private-sector management. Many public corporations have assumed that managers have no families, or, if they do, that wives and children are at the service of the corporation and have no interests which would be threatened by periodic uprooting. Movement between the industries could offer an alternative to periodic family upheavals.

What has been written on the role of management so far has stemmed from a straightforward appraisal of its role in socialised industry. Nothing that has been said could constitute a philosophy of management which is distinctly socialist. Could such a philosophy be formulated? The answer is probably yes, and two elements can be easily discerned. The first is the need to avoid discrimination against those who are not solely committed to the management system. The second is an internal attack on inflated salaries.

The first element may not appear to be particularly important. However, one traditional element in socialist thinking is the need for an individual to obtain self-fulfilment in a variety of ways. Orthodox management theory has always expected individuals to be managers first, second, and third, with no time available for anything else. Public corporations have been far in advance of their private sector counterparts in allowing managers to be active in political and social organisations, but even so some of their instructions could not be described as excessively liberal. Industry must be organised to allow the individual the flexibility to choose the life-style he wants.

The second element of 'socialist management', the attack on inflated salaries, is more obvious and less likely to be popular. However, the gulf in the standard of living between those at the top and those at the bottom of the pyramid in public sector organisation must be unacceptable to anyone with socialist values. Redistribution must take place at both ends to be effective. This idea will never gain universal acceptance, but that is no argument against a positive stance by those within the organisation who feel committed on this issue.

The consideration of socialist management brings out a view that has been present throughout the whole of the discussions of the last two chapters. The socialisation of 'public ownership' depends not just on legislative change from above, but also on the attitudes of the individuals operating in the broader industrial environment. This does not simply apply to management. A more positive response is also required from the workers, Government and local authorities.

What has been attempted in this chapter is to set out some guidelines for the debate. The need for public ownership has been established earlier in the book. The problems of socialising the system have been discussed at the Government, industry and employee levels and a number of necessary conditions for its successful operation have been examined. Many other problems remain to be identified, tackled and resolved. Since what is advocated is the establishment of an exploratory and evolving system of common ownership, this is scarcely surprising.

The importance of successful common ownership to the Labour Party cannot be overstated. There is considerable evidence to suggest that a lack of public confidence in nationalised industry has led to growing antagonism to Labour's industrial policy. An opinion poll undertaken by Opinion Research Centre and published in *The Times* on 13 January 1975 showed that 67 per cent of the

2000 workers in private industry sampled would oppose nationalisation of their firm and only 18 per cent would support it. A survey of 1900 adults in Britain carried out by Market and Opinion Research International and published in *The Economist* on 24 July 1976 showed that 76 per cent of those asked opposed plans for nationalisation of banking and insurance – and this was true of 63 per cent of Labour Party supporters questioned.

Of course these results represent in part a fear of change. One questions how many Rolls-Royce workers would have opposed nationalisation in 1971. Nevertheless the fact that the prospect of nationalisation leads to a hostile reaction from the workers in some of the industries concerned – the bank employees provide an example – should concern supporters of public ownership.

In the previous chapter it was argued that public ownership would inevitably grow as nationalisation was used as a repair mechanism for the failings of private ownership. The Labour Party believes that there is a strong political case for public ownership over and above the pragmatic one. Rarely has anyone argued that common ownership is simply a better way to run an industry, that the structures and organisation of common ownership could be inherently superior to those of private ownership. This book suggests that this is so, and common ownership can provide a solution to the industrial problems of an advanced society. The Labour Party must not forget that a policy for public ownership is a policy for managing, not just expanding, the public industrial sector.

Bibliography

The publications listed below are either cited in the text or likely to provide useful background material. The list is divided into four separate categories: 'Labour Politics and Nationalisation' covers the material presented in the first chapter; 'Nationalisation in the Post-war Years' the second; 'Industrial Democracy' the third. The final category, 'Aspects of Public Ownership', gives more detail on the sources of some of the arguments presented in the remainder of the book.

LABOUR POLITICS AND NATIONALISATION

Main sources cited are Annual Conference Reports of the Labour Representation Committee (1900–5), Labour Party Annual Conference Reports (1906–76) and Trades Union Congress Reports.

Labour Party publications
   Labour and the New Social Order (1918)
   Coal and Commonsense (1926)
   *Labour and the Nation (1928)
   For Socialism and Peace (1934)
   *Labour's Immediate Programme (1937)
   *Labour Believes in Britain (1949)
   Labour and the New Society (1950)
   Challenge to Britain (1953)
   Industry and Society (1957)
   Publi Enterprise (1957)
   Signpcosts for the Sixties (1961)
   Labour's Economic Strategy (1969)
   Economic Strategy, Growth and Unemployment (1971)
   *Labour's Programme for Britain (1972)
   The National Enterprise Board: Labour's State Holding Company (1973)
   Labour's Programme for Britain (1973)
   *Labour's Programme for Britain (1976)
                *major Party programmes, but not cited in text

Books, articles and pamphlets
   E. Eldon Barry, *Nationalisation in British Politics* (London: Jonathan Cape, 1965)
   David Butler and Anne Sloman, *British Political Facts 1900–1975* (London: Macmillan, 1975)
   G. D. H. Cole, *A History of the Labour Party from 1914* (London: Routledge & Kegan Paul, 1948)
   Margaret Cole (ed.), *The Webbs and their Work* (London: Frederick Muller, 1949)
   C. A. R. Crosland, *The Future of Socialism* (London: Jonathan Cape, 1956)
   Hugh Gaitskell, *Socialism and Nationalisation* (London: Fabian Society Tract No. 300, 1956)

A. H. Hanson, 'Labour and the Public Corporation,' *Public Administration* 23 (1954) 203–9.

Stephen Haseler, *The Gaitskellites* (London: Macmillan, 1969)

Stuart Holland (ed.), *The State as Entrepreneur* (London: Weidenfeld & Nicolson, 1972)

Stuart Holland, *The Socialist Challenge* (London: Quartet, 1975)

Robert McKenzie, *British Political Parties* (London: Heinemann, 1955)

Herbert Morrison, *Socialisation and Transport* (London: Constable, 1933)

Geoffrey Ostergaard, *Public Ownership in Great Britain* (unpublished thesis 1953, Oxford University)

M. V. Posner and S. K. Woolf, *Italian Public Enterprise* (London: Gerald Duckworth, 1967)

TUC, *Report on Public Control and Regulation of Industry and Trade* (London: 1932)

TUC, *Post War Reconstruction – Interim Report* (London: 1944)

Sidney and Beatrice Webb, *A Constitution for the Socialist Commonwealth of Great Britain* (London: London School of Economics, 1920)

NATIONALISATION IN THE POST-WAR YEARS

Most important sources are Annual Reports of the public corporations and periodic Parliamentary debates.

Acts of Nationalisation
   Coal Industry Nationalisation Act 1946
   Transport Act 1947
   Electricity Act 1947
   Gas Act 1948
   Iron and Steel Act 1949
   Iron and Steel Act 1967
   Post Office Act 1968
   Industry Act 1975 (established NEB)
   Petroleum and Submarine Pipe-lines Act 1975 (established BNOC)
   Aircraft and Shipbuilding Industries Act 1977

Government publications (all HMSO)
   Transport Policy, Cmd 8538 (1952)
   Report of the Committee on National Policy for the Use of Fuel and Power Resources (1952)
   Reorganisation of the Nationalised Transport Undertakings, Cmnd 1248 (1961)
   The Financial and Economic Obligations of the Nationalised Industries, Cmnd 1337 (1961)
   Fuel Policy, Cmnd 2798 (1965)
   Transport Policy, Cmnd 3057 (1966)
   Reorganisation of the Post Office, Cmnd 3233 (1967)
   Nationalised Industries: A Review of Economic and Financial Objectives, Cmnd 3437 (1967)
   Fuel Policy, Cmnd 3438 (1967)
   Railway Policy, Cmnd 3439 (1967)
   Transport of Freight, Cmnd 3470 (1967)

Ministerial Control of the Nationalised Industries, Cmnd 4027 (1969)
Relations with the Public, Cmnd 5067 (1972)
Capital Investment Procedures, Cmnd 6106 (1975)
Transport Policy: A Consultation Document, Vols I and II (1976)
Transport Policy, Cmnd 6836 (1977)
Report of the Working Group on a Co-operative Development Agency, Cmnd 6972 (1977)

Books, articles and pamphlets

Sir Norman Chester, *The Nationalisation of British Industry 1945–51* (London: HMSO, 1975)
A. H. Hanson (ed.), *Nationalisation: A Book of Readings* (London: Allen & Unwin, 1963)
C. Harlow, *Innovation and Productivity under Nationalisation* (London: PEP, Allen & Unwin, 1977)
R. Kelf-Cohen, *British Nationalisation 1945–73* (London: Macmillan, 1973)
National Economic Development Office, *A Study of UK Nationalised Industries* (London: 1976) – Main Report, Appendix Volume and the following Background Papers:
  1. *Financial Analysis*
  2. *Relationships of government and public enterprises in France, West Germany and Sweden*
  3. *Output, investment and productivity*
  4. *Manpower and pay trends*
  5. *Price behaviour*
  6. *Relationship with other sectors of the economy: the evidence of input-output analysis*
  7. *Exports and imports*
G. and P. Polanyi, 'The Efficiency of Nationalised Industries', *Moorgate and Wall Street Review*, spring 1972, 27–49
R. W. S. Pryke, *Public Enterprise in Practice* (London: MacGibbon & Kee, 1971)
R. W. S. Pryke and J. S. Dodgson, *The Rail Problem* (London: Martin Robertson, 1975)
G. Reid, K. Allen and D. J. Harris, *The Nationalised Fuel Industries* (London: Heinemann Educational Books, 1973)
Merlyn Rees, *The Public Sector in the Mixed Economy* (London: Batsford, 1973)
Select Committee on Nationalised Industries:
  1st Report Session 1967–8, *Ministerial Control of the Nationalised Industries*, HC371 (London: HMSO, 1968)
  2nd Report Session 1970–1, *Relations with the Public*, HC514 (London: HMSO, 1971)
  1st Report Session 1973–4, *Capital Investment Procedures*, HC65 (London: HMSO, 1973)
A. W. J. Thomson and L. C. Hunter, *The Nationalised Transport Industries* (London: Heinemann Educational Books, 1973)
L. Tivey (ed.), *The Nationalised Industries since 1960: A Book of Readings* (London: Allen & Unwin, 1973)

154   *Socialising Public Ownership*

INDUSTRIAL DEMOCRACY

Government publications (all HMSO)

Report of the Royal Commission on Trade Unions and Employers' Associations, Cmnd 3623 (1968)

Industrial Democracy: A Discussion Paper on Worker Participation in Harland and Wolff (Belfast: HMSO, 1975)

The Structure of the Electricity Supply Industry in England and Wales, Cmnd 6388 (1976)

Industrial Democracy: European Experience [background papers for Bullock prepared by E. Batstone and P. L. Davies] (1976)

Report of the Committee of Inquiry on Industrial Democracy [the Bullock Committee], Cmnd 6706 (1977) – including evidence, particularly of TUC, GMWU and EETPU

Books, articles and pamphlets

The Framework of Joint Consultation (London: Acton Society Trust, 1952)

T. Adizes, *Industrial Democracy: Yugoslav Style* (New York: Free Press, 1971)

C. Balfour (ed.), *Participation in Industry* (London: Croom Helm, 1973)

M. Barratt-Brown and S. Holland, *Public Ownership and Democracy* (IWC pamphlet No. 38)

P. Blumberg, *Industrial Democracy: The Sociology of Participation* (London: Constable, 1968)

P. Brannen, E. Batstone, D. Fatchett and P. White, *The Worker Directors* (London: Hutchinson, 1976)

Bristol Aircraft Workers, *A New Approach to Public Ownership* (IWC pamphlet No. 43)

H. Clegg, *Industrial Democracy and Nationalisation*: a study prepared for the Fabian Society (London: Blackwell, 1951)

H. Clegg, *A New Approach to Industrial Democracy* (London: Blackwell, 1960)

K. Coates and A. Topham, *Catching up with the Times: How Far the TUC Got the Message about Workers' Control* (IWC pamphlet No. 37)

K. Coates and A. Topham, *Industrial Democracy in Great Britain: A Book of Readings and Witnesses for Workers' Control* (London: MacGibbon & Kee, 1968)

K. Coates and A. Topham, *The New Unionism* (London: Peter Owen, 1972)

F. Emery and E. Thorstud, *Form and Content in Industrial Democracy* (London: Tavistock, 1969)

Labour Party, *Industrial Democracy: Working Party Report* (London: 1967)

J. Obradovic, 'Workers Participation: Who Participates,' *Industrial Relations* XIV (1975) 32–44

M. Poole, *Workers' Participation in Industry* (London: Routledge & Kegan Paul, 1975)

G. Radice (ed.), *Working Power* (London: Fabian Society Tract No. 431, 1974)

E. Roberts, *Workers' Control* (London: Allen & Unwin, 1973)

H. Scanlon, *The Way Forward for Workers' Control* (IWC pamphlet No. 1)

F. Singleton and T. Topham, *Workers' Control in Yugoslavia* (London: Fabian Society pamphlet No. 233, 1968)

TUC, *Public Ownership: An Interim Report* (London: 1953)

TUC, *Industrial Democracy: Interim Report* (London: 1973)

TUC, *Industrial Democracy* (London: 1974)

ASPECTS OF PUBLIC OWNERSHIP

Background to Case Studies
1. Rolls-Royce
   John Argenti, *Corporate Collapse* (London: McGraw-Hill, 1976)
   Department of Trade, *Rolls-Royce Ltd* (London: HMSO, 1973)
   Robert Gray, *Rolls on the Rocks* (London: Compton Press, 1971)
   Rolls-Royce and the RB211 Aero-Engine, Cmnd 4860 (London: HMSO, 1972)
2. The British Steel Industry
   Reports by the British Iron and Steel Federation and the Joint Iron Council to the Ministry of Supply, Cmd 6811 (London: HMSO, 1946)
   Richard Pryke, *Why Steel* (London: Fabian Research Series No. 248, 1965)
   The Steel Industry – The Stage I Report of the Development Co-ordinating Committee of the British Iron and Steel Federation (London: British Iron and Steel Federation, 1966)
   British Steel Corporation: Ten Year Development Strategy, Cmnd 5226(London: HMSO, 1973)
   Young Fabian Steel Group, *Crisis in Steel* (London: Young Fabian Pamphlet No. 38, 1974)
   David Heal, *The Steel Industry in Post-war Britain* (London: David and Charles, 1974)
   John Vaizey, *The History of British Steel* (London: Weidenfeld & Nicolson, 1974)
3. The Motor-cycle Co-operative
   Ken Coates (ed.), *The New Worker Co-operatives* (Nottingham: Spokesman Books, 1976)
   Regular articles in the *Workers' Control Bulletin* (published by the Institute for Workers' Control)
   Strategy Alternatives for the British Motorcycle Industry, HC532 (London: HMSO, 1975)

Books, articles and pamphlets
   Stafford Beer, *Platform for Change* (London: John Wiley, 1975)
   Milton Friedman, *Capitalism and Freedom* (Chicago: University of Chicago Press, 1962)
   Milton Friedman, *From Galbraith to Economic Freedom* (London: Institute of Economic Affairs, 1977)
   J. K. Galbraith, *Economics and the Public Purpose* (London: André Deutsch, 1974)
   J. K. Galbraith, 'The Economic Problems of the Left', *New Statesman* (20 February 1976) 218
   Lisl Klein, *New Forms of Work Organisation* (London: Cambridge University Press, 1976)
   E. J. Mishan, *The Costs of Economic Growth* (London: Penguin Books, 1967)
   National Consumer Council, *Consumers and the Nationalised Industries* (London: HMSO, 1976)
   National Consumer Council, *Industrial Democracy and Consumer Democracy: Seven Reasons Why the TUC is Wrong* (London: 1977)
   S. J. Prais, *The Evolution of Giant Firms in Britain* (London: Cambridge University Press, 1977)
   J. R. Wildsmith, *Managerial Theories of the Firm* (London: Martin Robertson, 1973)

Index

DATE DUE